THE WELL-STOCKED AND GILDED CAGE

LAWRENCE LENHART

ESSAYS

Outpost19 | San Francisco
outpost19.com

Lenhart, Lawrence
        The Well-Stocked and Gilded Cage / Lawrence
Lenhart
        ISBN 9781944853013 (pbk)

Library of Congress Control Number: 2016910709

These essays have appeared or are forthcoming in *Alaska Quarterly Review, Gulf Coast, Prairie Schooner, Fourth Genre, Guernica, Passages North, Fourteen Hills, Wag's Revue, Terrain, JuxtaProse, SunDog Lit,* and *BOAAT.*

"Give Me That For Nothing, Now I Am Going Away" (originally published in *Wag's Revue*) was selected as a notable essay in Best American Essays 2015.

"Of No Ground: Late Days In the Country of Eighteen Tides," earned *Terrain*'s 6th Annual Creative Nonfiction Award.

"The Well-Stocked and Gilded Cage" won *Prairie Schooner's* 2016 Virginia Faulkner Award for Excellence in Writing.

When necessary, names have been altered. When serviceable, time has been compressed.

OUTPOST19

ORIGINAL
PROVOCATIVE
READING

THE WELL-STOCKED AND GILDED CAGE

for Arni and Windsor

Table of Contents

Give Me That For Nothing, Now I Am Going Away

I.

I go with her to burgle her childhood home. We drive past the house twice, once from each direction, ensuring that the driveway is empty. A Jeepless house is a fatherless house. Continuing a half-mile north of her old stomping grounds, we turn onto Lindy Farm Road, thudding in and out of ruts. I didn't know before today that she was capable of silence. I decide on a shadowy spot off the berm and pull over. This is where we'll park, conceal, and ditch the car. I cover my SUV with branches, some brush. It's amateur hour. It's sunset.

We stride parallel with barn beams, electric cow fences, strips of shingles from the shingleless eaves. We move in fallow cornrow gutters. I remember her saying that this is where the arrowheads are embedded in the watershed's soil. Susquehannock artifacts. There was a phase when she joined her dad to collect the arrowheads; a phase before Lindy, whose farm is adjacent to the housing development, joined the Pennsylvania No-Till Alliance (2008); a phase before she learned the word "domicile," before she ran away (2005); a phase before the age-of-onset for her father's mental illness (2004), but not much before.

In the field, I am feeling detectable, highly visible in flannel. I notice all the vantages from which I can be noticed. The backs of houses. Over thirty windows. I think how one must have a set of eyes. I settle on the weathervane as narc. A cockerel skewered to a cricking axis, facing away from us. Its rust-red cockscomb. I point it out to her, but she doesn't look. We are marching now, single-filed, the garbage bags flapping from our pockets.

A breeze sends honeysuckle. I watch for the cockerel to turn on us, but its pivot is immobilized by rust. When I convulse in sneezes, she turns around and puts her hands up like, What

1

do I do with you? How many times I've said "allergy season" this season. Near her father's house, behind a tangle of grape-bearing vines, we lose the swagger.

Moments like these—standing on cement driveway while she pokes at potential garage door codes—I remember a hide-and-seek truth: visibility has as much to do with time as it does space. A few seconds can feel like an hour under the floodlights.

I whisper at her back. "What's wrong? Isn't the code working?" Apparently, he's changed it, a personal insult to her because the code was her birth date (0-3-1-9). Later, she'll mention how the old code made access to that house seem like a birthright.

Once we're in (the code is now his birth date)—the garage door tri-folding up, then down—we hurry to calm the dog, a setter. Jericho stops barking when he sees her.

"So big," she says to Jericho. "So big now." It's been decades in dog years since she's seen him.

I look around the kitchen at mail strewn on a laminate island, its uncleared dishes, a rice seasoning packet, purpled wine glasses, new fishing licenses, notepad scribble, a coil bracelet keychain, a water bottle lid, a rebate check with a sticky note on it (*Before Jan*). There are custom magnets on the refrigerator from DelMarVa beaches, a nephew's graduation photo, and a demijohn of homemade wine. I can see the porch through the front room windows, the welcome mat I've bypassed. My sympathetic nervous system (fight-or-flight) is wholly engaged.

"We should hurry," I say to her.

She is still leaning over Jericho, tugging at scruffs of red mane, his panting accelerating, tongue dripping onto her sandals. She nods, but I can see she's calm. Her being home is likely having the opposite effect on her. Her body is telling her rest, digest.

"Oh cool," she says, noticing the demijohn. "He made wine this fall."

She opens a cabinet, carefully selects a Disney mug, and fills it with wine. She glugs. "Hoo!" She coughs and raises her eyebrows. "It's way strong."

She offers it to me, and I carry it, following her to the base-ment.

Months ago, when she glimpsed my cross country trophies on display in my house and said that she didn't have any of those sentimentally-charged childhood items because they are all in boxes in her father's basement, I suggested: "Well, we should fucking steal 'em back." I didn't expect to be taken so literally.

II.

The Vocabula Mahakuassica is the extant volume of words and phrases comprising the extinct Susquehannock language. It is a diminutive lexicon compiled by Swedish missionary John Campanius in the 1640s. Of the scant 89 words and phrases recorded, the preserved language alternates between utilitarian bartering and conviviality.

> *Kaatzie. Testa sis chijerw. Tzátzie, jihadaeaero.* Come here.
> The dog does not bite. Sit and stay, my particularly good friend.

Katzha gaije? Tinnijgo otthohwrha? Chotsis chijrw. What have you got?
How much money will you have for it? See here what I will give you.

> *Agaendeero. Chanooro hiss.* We are
> good friends. I make much of you.

>> *Kareenach testa hije gaijw.* I have a knife for you.
>> *Kassha schaeaenu.* Give me that for nothing.
>> *Taesta, taesta.* No, no.

Hoona sattaande.
Now I am going away.

One June morning, her mother moved out of the house, packing and leaving so very quietly.

"She was too dignified to make a scene. Can you imagine

[my mother], like wailing or curling up on a carpet? I don't think so."

I ask her if her mother said goodbye to her. "I think so," she says. "I definitely remember her saying goodbye to Jericho, though. That was sad. He was *hers*." After a quick middle finger at her husband, her mother's last words in the house, maybe to the house: "Too bad." It was the last time all three of them would share a room, excepting a courtroom for custody and a gymnasium for graduation.

"What about your father?" I ask. She shakes her head. "I woke up," she says, "well, I didn't really sleep that first night Mom was gone. When I looked out my bedroom [window] in the morning, though, my dad was doing target archery in the yard with my mom's pillows. She had these like, oversized pillows that Dad hated." I ask her what color they were. "Mauve?" she said. I imagine the pillows sitting on lawn chairs, clefting in the middle like a slumping heart, her father a deranged Cupid.

That fall, her father began studying the *Vocabula Mahakuassica*. He liked the idea that if he could just commit 89 words to memory, he could absurdly claim mastery of an entire language. Those days, when she came home from school, Jericho would rush her as she removed her shoes, and her father would say, "Testa sis chijerw" (the dog does not bite). If she came home from the skate hop at 1 a.m. instead of midnight, her father would unlock the door with a "Serwquacksi" (you are bad). He made copies of the *Vocabula Mahakuassica* for her, for the widower next door, for the Lindy farm boys, for Lindy himself, but nobody would match his zeal. Some days, the only words her father spoke to her were in Susquehannock. When he asked her something in Susquehannock, an exaggerated rising inflection lingering between them, she replied with the only phrase she cared to learn: "Taesta zwroncka" (I don't understand).

On the days Lindy rototilled his land—six teeth per gang stirring and pulverizing the soil—she'd accompany her father to the fields to look for arrowheads. The tillage unburied chips of flint, bodkin points shaped like rose petals, pink or orange or gray. Sometimes they were lucky and found kill sites where Indians scraped meat from hides, and the ground was littered with a half-dozen arrowheads or more. Lindy didn't mind them looting arrowheads so long as Jericho didn't harass his chickens.

"I bet you Lindy's granddad knew the language," her father would say. "They're Swedes just like John was." He spoke of John Campanius, missionary-cum-lexicographer, as a would-be companion.

I don't broach the irony that her father was quasi-fluent in this dead language while the only English words he ever practiced to his ex-wife were "cow" and "pig" and "ungrateful bitch."

III.

In the bassinet (twenty years assembled), beneath a blanket (threadbare yellow yarn), in a tackle box (its cascading trays), she runs her fingers through dozens of arrowheads. The flint trickles like she is a brook, as if she is a current, a ström (Swedish for "stream").

"Hoona sattaande," she says to me.

I look at her. *Hoona sattaande?*

"I remember that one," she says. "He'd say it before leaving. It means leaving or something."

"You want to leave?" I ask encouragingly.

"Hoona sattande," she repeats.

"I thought you wanted trophies," I remind her. The garbage bags are still empty.

The trophies are in a corrugated box for an artificial Christmas tree. I find them wrapped individually in newspaper—crosswords and classifieds, Sudoku and comics crumpled around the gold-plastic figurines, medals dangling from their napes. She staggers them in a row, counts them like she used to. Most are swimming trophies. Each figurine looks as if it might dive from its marble promontory and onto basement cement.

As she massages one of the figurines, she says, "I think I'm going to leave the trophies. Did you taste the wine?"

I haven't. I'm paranoid about leaving my DNA on the mug, but she watches expectantly, so I tilt an ounce or more down my throat and cough louder than she had.

"Shiiit," I say stupidly. "It's like moonshine wine."

We are surrounded by woven baskets brimming with Beanie Babies, Furbies, Cabbage Patch Kids, Little Ponies, Treasure Trolls, and a forlorn Pound Puppy called Jericho Too. There are transparent Tupperware containers with pog discs and voodoo sticks, laser pointers and puzzles, Sega Wires tangled with Skip It, a Gameboy crusted with Gak, kneepads and goggles, a long-dead chartreuse digital pet Tamagotchi ("friend" in Japanese).

I peer inside the Easy Bake Oven. "There are still brownie crumbs in here." I laugh.

She is emptying the arrowheads from the tackle box, manically filling her large purse. Her age fluctuates as she uses her hands like trowels, a palm's worth scooped with each sweep. She is a child or she is grown. It's uncertain warpath play. When the top tray compartments are empty, she pries the box further to reveal a second and third tray. She empties these too. Beneath all is a larger compartment: in it an ancient shank to which Indians affixed the arrowheads.

"Oh my God," she says, ignoring the shank, instead removing a glass jar. Lifting it meekly, bringing it near to her face, her right eye magnified by convex glass, she seems devastated by all the teeth.

"Are those Native American teeth?" I ask, again feeling dumb.

"I think they're mine," she says, rotating the jar. For a moment, I think she might put them back in her mouth. "It's so creepy," she says.

I stand above her and scratch my fingers across her shoulder blade to her spine. I mean for it to be comforting, but instead it feels vaguely anthropological.

"Hoona sattande," she says. We take turns finishing the wine, say goodbye to Jericho, go.

It feels unnatural to simply walk away from a burglary, so we run instead. I've got her purse. She handles the jar. Arrowheads click against arrowheads, teeth against teeth. The cornfield still smells like honeysuckle as the cockerel directs us north. Across the fallow rows we trek, gaining velocity. We are feeling like field mice. She even squeaks a couple times in excitement.

Halfway to the farm road where I've parked my SUV, she reaches into her purse, still slung over my shoulder, and she chucks handfuls of arrowheads, bodkin-pointed, as if restocking the field. I throw them too, hear them anchoring to the soil, but imagine them slipping through the morass, to mantle and crust. The people of the muddy river—proto-Iroquoians once cruelly likened to savage stalks—are reunited with their shank tips. She throws teeth too, and I see them land: hard white specks on brown earth. When the last tooth is gone, all of her removed from her father's house, her escape becomes euphoric.

In the car, staring into her lap, refusing to look in the rear-view mirror, where I see what could be any farm in the Susquehanna Valley, she turns the jar over in her hand. When I speed to 65 mph, she lets it fly and fracture off an oak tree.

Dogsucker:
The Written Oral

Bullfucker (continued): forte

Either way, she fucked the bull. Not even she would deny it. As evidence, see her chimera son the Minotaur, half-man half-bull. Her husband Minos consulted with the oracles, and the Minotaur was incarcerated in Daedalus's Labyrinth. And what would you do if you were Minos? If your wife (called Pasiphaë) lusted after a snow-white bull, copulated with it, birthed a monster, and brought shame upon your already tragic—like the Kennedys, but Greek—family line?

Or rather, the bull fucked her. Pasiphaë recruited the famed Athenian artificer Daedalus to trick the sexualized bull into mating with her. Daedalus cleverly constructed a hollow heifer with a hide façade. In Rebecca Armstrong's *Cretan Women*, an outraged Minos regards the invention as a pimpish contraption rather than a product of carpentry.

As with Icarus's wings, there are no historical blueprints for the invention, but if you really think about it—in explicit detail as I have—the design can be inferred from just about any illustration in bovine animal husbandry. The thing about a pimped-out proxy bull is that within the hollow body of the wooden heifer, Pasiphaë is on all fours herself, her violet himation and loincloth pulled up and over her hips, her vagina hovering near a carefully whittled hole through which the bull's penis may poke. The diameter of an erect bull penis is seven centimeters while the diameter of the average female vagina is around two centimeters. You'll have to excuse my fascination with the literality of myth.

Why, Daedalus? Why enable her infamous adultery? While Armstrong offers several explanations, I prefer her notion that

Daedalus had an "amoral, detached fascination with the solving of technical problems."

And this bull—object of lust, fucker of cavities in wooden heifers, impregnator of Cretan Queen Pasiphaë, father of the concealed Minotaur—from whence did it come? Minos had prayed to Poseidon for a symbol that would make apparent his right to claim the throne of Crete, and Poseidon obliged. He garnered Minos with the snowy bull that manifested in the breakers of some Mediterranean beach. O, Minos: careful what you wish for.

Dogsucker (continued): forte

By Christmas 1998, I was convinced that my sophisticated pleas would finally yield a dog—a small hypoallergenic terrier—please please can we please? I made my parents feel blameworthy for isolating me; not only was I siblingless, but also woefully enrolled at a small and distant parochial school, Queen of Angels. I was certain that on that Christmas morning, I would awake to adorable yipping, a puppy trembling in shallow backyard snow, that I would point at it and ask my parents if it was mine, and when they said yes, I would spontaneously name it and call it inside. Instead, though, I received a slap-in-the-face virtual pet Tamagotchi.

Tamagotchi is a small egg-shaped keychain computer, a species of digital pet created in Japan in 1996 for parents in small city apartments, or those with shithead kids who had not been able to sustain the illusion that they could take on the responsibilities of pet ownership in the weeks leading up to Christmas. Tamagotchi pet owners are required to feed, interact, and discipline their pets to encourage them into the next stage of development, a Piagetian precursor to Pokémon. To achieve this, there were three rubber buttons below the screen display.

There was a hazy satisfaction associated with Tamagotchi play, but I craved the real thing. I craved the analog pet—fur and skin and ligament and bone, hot breath, bad breath, pink tongue, claws on ceramic, tail like a joystick, goop in the corners of the eyes, unpredictable fits of energy, catatonic until sparrow lands on window sill or until jay bustles in chimney flue or rabbits nibble at backyard rosebushes, whatever other sudden alarms turn a ball of fur into a kamikaze pinball.

When Tamagotchi's 1.5-volt alkaline battery cells were toast come March/come April, I didn't ask for replacements. I put the egg to rest in a drawer with other childhood distractions.

Bullfucker (continued): madness

Poseidon gifted the snowy bull to Minos, and the bull acted as a symbol that Minos should inherit the Cretan throne. With his electoral talisman, Minos swiftly became King Minos. Rather than sacrifice the bull back to Poseidon, though, as Minos knew he ought do, Minos in his supreme megalomania had become so attached to the bull—this arbiter of his royalty—that he instead sacrificed one hundred ordinary cows. Poseidon, a megalomaniac himself, was understandably insulted by the offering.

It's like when your dad lets you take the Blue Corvette to Norwin High School Senior Prom. He says, "Go ahead. I'll take the old Camry for the night." What a great dad. And you take a high school sweetheart to the confluence of the three rivers: the Allegheny, the Monongahela, and the Ohio. You take pictures in the car, beside the car, on the car. You're even wearing an electron blue vest to match the 50th anniversary paintjob. And even though your high school does not designate a king and queen at the end of the night (they think it promotes the very social hierarchy they've been trying for four years to defeat), the car has boosted your ego enough that you are the *de facto* king. And when prom is over, and you've accelerated the Corvette into the triple digits on desolate parkway stretches from Pittsburgh to suburban Irwin (don't tell Dad, though), eventually parking it in your driveway late at night or early in the morning, and the next day, you are hungover, and your dad asks how the night was, how the Corvette was, and you give a thumbs up, and when he asks for the keys back, you tell him, "No, Dad. Why don't you keep the Camry?"

Here's where myth multiplies.

An irate Poseidon punishes Minos. At least this is what is emphasized in the Roman poet Virgil's *Eclogue VI* ('Bucolic VI'). The punishment: Minos can keep the snow-white bull, the only caveat being that his old lady, Pasiphaë, will be afflicted with an intense lovesickness for the bull. She will be forlorn, out of sorts, until she copulates with it.

Enough of the conflict between Poseidon and Minos, though. Let us consider Pasiphaë. Pasiphaë is the object of Virgil's sincere and constant sympathy. Virgil recognizes Poseidon as bully and Minos as culprit, how their egomania victimizes Pasiphaë (*a, uirgo infelix*), and she has no choice but to climb the foothills—of Mount Ida, was it?—as if she is a herdsman. She is in want of the bull. An ensemble translation of *Eclogue VI* would catalogue her torment thusly: Poseidon induces Pasiphaë's mania. *A, uirgo infelix.* Pasiphaë looks for the bull's tracks, follows the hoof prints up and down hillocks, becoming a feral wife—no, amatorfauna. She solicits the Nymphs to close off the groves in order to keep the bull near. She drives heifers to stable. Away with competition! And when Pasiphaë (*a, uirgo infelix*) finds him, his snowy hide reclining amongst hyacinths, she climbs into Daedalus's contraption, and when she is finally, finally his inamorata, finally, finally mounted, bull-fucked, sated, the poet Virgil asks Pasiphaë, "*A! uirgo infelix quae te dementia cepit?*" 'Ah! Poor maiden, where have your wits flown?'

By emphasizing the 'madness,' Virgil's attitude towards Pasiphaë's *turpis concubitus*, or 'shameful union,' is similar to that of Sigmund Freud. In Freud's 1905 essay, "Sexual Aberrations," one of the conditions in which an individual may engage in bestial relations—aside from cowardice or impotence—is "an urgent instinct (one which will not allow of postponement)" and only if the individual "cannot at [that] moment get possession of any more appropriate object." While Freud's psychology is pursuant of etiology, Virgil's poetry is a pledge of compassion to his subject. Both, though, are aware of the urgent instinct.

Aphrodite liaises for Poseidon, afflicts Pasiphaë with this instinct—almost as if by an osmotic spritz of a love potion, some progesterone-infused lustral water—and Pasiphaë becomes the unwitting offender of not just adultery, but zoophilia as well. Armstrong dubs it an "isolating transgression."

Dogsucker (continued)

On Christmas Eve, just eight days before the new millennium, we picked up a small Yorkshire Terrier. You've likely seen this breed in Victorian paintings wearing a red bow, looking prim. You should know: Grizz was bowless, macho. That night, Grizz stayed in the Pet Taxi on my dresser, eye-level with my bed. Even though I wasn't supposed to take him out until morning, I opened the cage every so often and cradled him. Most of the night, we blinked at each other, his eyes two orange flecks of tapetum lucidum, little round flames of tissue coated in the oil of his tears.

Grizz and I were inseparable that spring. When I got home from Queen of Angels, I sprinted from the bus stop to my room, changed out of my knit vest and khakis—if I didn't, they'd call me Preppy Pussy (Pee Pee for short)—and put on something public-school-looking. I soaked my gelled hair under the sink's gush, leashed Grizz, and took backyard shortcuts to the public school bus stop. Grizz was a good walker. He had a tendency to venture ahead, but there was always some slack in the leash. He wasn't the kind of territorial scatterbrain who would sniff and leglift at every fence and mailbox post on the street. We stomped over fresh-mowed lawns riddled with crabgrass and clover and dandelions, past Japanese maple trees and hollyhocks, relished our suburban azimuth to the bus stop intersection.

Even though I went to a private school, there was nothing

more impossibly private than the thirty-six-foot public school bus with its closed or half-closed windows muffling cacophony, depicting unfamiliar sneering faces, scalps pinwheeled against the glass, the variety of acne pocks and four-eyed, black-teed, polo-collared, boyfriend/girlfriend manacled hand-holders, limbs slung over seat backs, back-seat tyrants, homework head-starters, headphone headbobbers, last-second seatshufflers. I knew nothing of this variety at Queen of Angels.

I stood in the Garasy's driveway, flanked by mailbox and Grizz, and for a few seconds, just before the driver engaged the door's lever, everyone on the bus looked down at me, like *Who the fuck?* They rarely tried to interact with me except for the one time when the eighth grader Rushner, who wore black contacts with white X pupils, spat out of his window, me as his intended target. Instead, the spit landed on the concrete, and I had to yank Grizz away so that he didn't lap it up.

From the bus stop, I'd go with my friends to a driveway, shoot basketball, and between buoyant smacks of rubber off cement—each smack obscuring valuable terminology for a boy eager to learn the parlance of the public school—they'd utter words like *fellatio* and its crude synonyms: *blow job, BJ, head, dome, suck off, deep throat, pole smoke, etc.*

Dogsucker (continued): epōnumos

For the first twelve years of my life, they called me Larry. And then, one day, they started calling me Dogsucker.

Years later, friends would introduce me to their friends as "This is Larry," followed by the brief intriguing epithet. The onus was then on me to reverse-engineer the epithet, to make the story more comprehensible to the skeptic. I'd wait for a re-action—shock, sympathy, confusion, outrage—and craft a con-gruous response. If he or she had the time, I'd tell the whole story.

Here's how it happened: Rushner, an oafish eight grader

with these demon-like contacts, got off the bus prematurely; his assigned stop was on Charles Drive, not Christine. He asked me, "Can I help you walk your dog?" I nodded. I didn't need the help. The generosity was absurd. It was just some naïve notion I had that maybe Rushner had a soft spot for dogs like I did. That maybe Rushner was one of those shithead kids whose parents thought couldn't handle the responsibilities of dog ownership. Did he too once get stuck with Tamagotchi? I gave Rushner the leash forthwith.

And he took off.

Even though he was fairly obese, Rushner had to have been running twice as fast as Grizz. At first, it looked like exercise. I laughed nervously. With some distance, though, it looked like theft. Then, when Grizz could no longer keep up, when there was no slack in the leash at all and my dog was somersaulting through the air, yelping, each yelp coinciding with his five-pound body bouncing off the asphalt like a furry deflated basketball, draggled past each lot—then, it seemed like torture.

Years later, Rushner shot himself in the stomach by accident. Years later, he was placed in a juvenile facility. Years later, he set a barn on fire. Years later, he shot his mother with a semiautomatic paintball gun in the parking lot of Giant Eagle. Years later, he turned into a Juggalo and publicly freestyled to Insane Clown Posse. I realize these are unfair details to include, and I am making him impossibly unsympathetic, but this is my first attempt at making a record of why they called me Dogsucker, and I am not at all at ease. I succumb to mythologizing Rushner because his story is inextricable with mine.

I was the first to catch up with Rushner and Grizz. My friends trotted closely behind. Grizz was lying on his side, not making a sound, bones possibly fractured. His rib cage went up and down, his diaphragm seeming to deflate more than it could inflate. His torso looked like it would explode or collapse entirely from the exhaustion. I didn't know what to say to Rushner, except "What the fuck!" and I was crying, though tearless, because I was panicking: the leash was still in Rushner's hand.

He smirked, and when I reached for the leash, he grabbed me by the throat and pushed me backward by my trachea like a WWE stunt he had seen on television. We were in the Tersey's yard, but it felt like we were standing on a precipice, on a cliff.

Thom told Rushner to give me the leash. "Quit fucking around, Rushner."

Rushner didn't even have to shake his head for me to know it was not going to be that easy. I could tell he was scheming because of the way his eyes were slit, concealing the villainous X contacts.

Rushner replied, "Larry has to suck its dick first."

Thom snorted, but when he understood Rushner's seriousness, his head shook slightly, and he became still. He realized what was at stake.

I looked at Rushner, kind of winced. I couldn't apprehend the underlying motivation. "Just give it to me," I said simply, hand extended for the leash.

Rushner strode backwards, dragging my already exhausted dog across the lawn, again towards the street. Grizz didn't even try to stand.

"I'll keep going," Rushner forewarned.

There's a moment in *Silence of the Lambs* when Buffalo Bill bellows to his hostage in the well, "Don't you hurt my dog!" The hostage, Catherine, clutches at the little Bichon Frise. "Don't you make me hurt your dog!" The reversibility of power can inspire courage.

I tried to tackle Rushner, tried to intercept the leash from his sausage fingers, but he pinched my trachea, and it felt instantly bruised.

"Suck it," he said, inadvertently reciting Steve Austin's slogan from D-Generation X WWE wrestling.

I looked at my friends. No guidance. I looked at Grizz, realized we were both hostages like on the first night with the Pet Taxi on the dresser when I wanted to take him out of the cage, and he wanted to be taken out. Recording this now, I remember how badly I had wanted a dog, how I thought there was no depth to the bargaining with my parents, how many times I must have said, *If you get me a dog, I'll...* I stood inside of that ellipsis, felt the grisly floor of my desperation, and reified myself as the guarantor of my dog's survival.

Without more protest, I scooped up my dog and felt his ribs expanding in my hands. Grizz could not catch his breath. I looked at him, just held him at eye-level for a few seconds before I lifted him a little higher. I searched Rushner's eyes for relent. There was none. I opened my mouth, and I put the small shaft of tissue inside. It felt like a small cigar, a fur cigarillo. After a few seconds, I felt the leash drop to the grass. Rushner let go in order to hunch into laughter.

He said, "I can't believe you just sucked your dog's dick. You fuggin' faggity ass!"

And I wasn't sure why he couldn't believe it because he was the one who had commanded it. *De*manded it. I started speed walking toward my house, heard Rushner's uncontrollable laughter at my back. I ignored my friends' petitions. In the closed garage, I sat with Grizz in my dad's Corvette, waiting for our parasympathetic nervous systems to engage. The phone rang, but I stayed silent, stuporous as I brushed the fur of Grizz's nape.

Dogsucker (continued)

In the University of Arizona library, with six tabs open on my browser, ranging from a documentary on zoophilia (*Zoo*, 2007) to Google Images of gargoyle chimeras to zoomed-and-pixelated cattle cocks on Oklahoma State University's Agricultural website, I become suddenly self-conscious as an undergraduate sits beside me. He has Greek letters stitched to his hoodie. I should know all the letters by now, but I don't. I minimize my browser window, only to reveal a Word document with the inconvenient header 'Dogsucker' (left) and 'Lenhart' (right). I am trying to avoid becoming the subject of fraternity and sorority rumormongers, cruel contemporary Greek mythologers.

I hastily save, realize my record is still classified, unfit for public, meant to be composed in private study corrals only. For now.

Bullfucker (continued): badness

Too bad for Pasiphaë, though, that Virgil's bucolic and sympathetic poem—an apologia for her madness—is not the only existing narrative of her tryst with the bull. Nor is it the most prominent. In Thomas Heywood's translation of *Ars Amatoria* ('Art of Love'), Roman poet Ovid writes: *"Pasiphae fieri gaudebat adultera tauri"* ('Pasiphaë took pleasure in becoming an adulteress with a bull'), and her reputation is forever tarnished. Unlike Virgil's mild Eclogues, Ovid's account of Pasiphaë appears in the sensationalist instruction manual for male and female relations, including such trite and universal wisdom as "don't forget her birthday" and "never ask her age," these gender roles pronounced even in the second year *anno domini*. However, Ovid's more complicated misogynistic defamation of Pasiphaë, which warns that women are more lustful than men and should be held accountable for their lustful actions, lays the groundwork for the double standard of the harlot. Ovid's warning to Minos is vicariously extended to all Roman men. It emphasizes the voluntariness of her action and does not forgive her as Virgil's *Eclogue VI* does.

This ancient slut shaming reduces the nuanced episode to a pastoral booty call. While the snowy white bull was called an *iuuencus* (young bull) in Virgil's account, it is instead called a *Taurus* (adult bull) in Ovid's. Subtle choices in diction provoke the sensationalist imagination.

For most people who heard my story secondhand, there was an assumption that Grizz was a big dog—a Labrador, a St. Bernard, a Great Dane—thereby maximizing the grotesqueness. They were later surprised that he was, in fact, a six-pound Yorkshire Terrier, which somehow made the event more defensible and less erotic. And too, the fact that Grizz was not erect—no pink lipstick—was redemptive.

The recurring anaphora from *Eclogues* ('Ah! Poor maiden')
is displaced in Heywood's translation of *Ars Amatoria*. Instead,
there is a scathing indictment of Pasiphaë's actions, an unjust
mockery:

> *If* Minos *please thee, no adulterer seeke thee,*
> *Or if thy husband* Minos *do not like thee,*
> *But thy lascivious thoughts are still increast,*
> *Deceive him with a man, not with a beast.*

Armstrong points out Ovid's is the "all too observant eye of the
social critic" as he brings attention to her "adulterous breath" as
she "plays harlot with a bull." If, in Ovid's estimation, Pasiphaë
acted out of voluntary lust, not as the subservient subject of
Poseidon's vengeance against Minos, then it opens the door to
the irreversible stigma of paraphilia.

While paraphilic acts may include pervasive "spanking,
whipping, cutting, binding, or strangulating," the *Diagnostic and
Statistical Manual of Mental Disorders, Fifth Edition*, also specifies
anomalous sexual interest in "children, corpses, or amputees…
as well as intense or preferential interest in nonhuman animals,
such as horses or dogs, or in inanimate objects, such as shoes or
articles made of rubber."

Once, in Tijuana, not far from the red light district,
hubbub of Mexican vice, four kilometers away from Paseo de
los Héroes, where I was to meet a friend for mezcal, I asked the
cab driver if there was really such a thing as a Tijuana Donkey
Show. He made a dramatic u-turn. His wheels were turning. He
had a specific destination in mind. I had to explain to him, "I
don't want to go. I just want to know if there is such a thing."
He made a less dramatic u-turn back toward the original destination and said with a sigh, "No. Actually no." I still wonder
what would have happened had we not boomeranged back, had
I ditched my friend for the company at the inevitable brothel.
Who was this girl onto whom the driver was prepared to project

the donkey myth, this fabricated exhibit of the Latina Pasiphaë?

The fallout, resulting from Pasiphaë's besmirched reputation: 1) Minos becomes "justifiably" bitter with his wife; 2) He bastardizes her "sire," the Minotaur and jails him in the impassable labyrinth; 3) Pasiphaë's daughter, Ariadne, in Ovid's *Heroides*, is shamed by her mother's perversion. And Pasiphaë, daughter of Helios, goes out like a flame.

Dogsucker (continued)

The shorter version of my story is: In seventh grade, Larry sucked his dog's dick. This is the version of the story that spread in the public middle schools. Maybe it's because hallway stories, or on-the-go stories, have to be economical. Maybe because that's all there really was to it. Why preamble when the route to taboo was so direct? Why justify such an inglorious action?

For weeks and weeks, my name underwent a metamorphosis—from Larry to Dogsucker. It sounded like an ill-advised superhero name. The compound nickname was whispered in the hallways of Middle School East and Middle School West. I had a sudden appreciation for the privacy of Queen of Angels. My class of forty-some peers knew nothing about my bus stop transgression. They were oblivious to my new humility. Years before, for example, Alaina and Alexis had inoculated me during a parking lot recess at Sacred Heart Church. They were arbiters of who was or wasn't passable, playing doctor and administering cooties shots en masse to the boys. The boys without immunization became temporary social pariahs. I was honored to have my skin circle-circle-dot-dotted. I horripilated in gratitude.

I was not entirely severed from the public middle school, though. I had a public school girlfriend at the time named Pearl. In order to get to Pearl's house, I had to walk back roads—shortcuts and accidental longcuts. I jog the route now—Christmas morning, twelve years later—with a pedometer. It measures 2.4 miles each way. It was always worth the trek because when her father wasn't home, she let me kiss her with tongue.

When he was home, though, we played soccer in the alley, never taking advantage of breakaways despite many opportunities; instead, we liked to keep the footwork tight, a close radius, so that when she defended, our helixing hips evoked grinding, which was permissible at public school dances. (At Q of A, we had to "leave room for the Holy Spirit.") There were a few blind spots beside the carport or by the neighbor's fence where Pearl and I could escape for a few minutes without the paternal sentry of Oak Av's alley.

In these blind spots, she would sometimes let me see her thong. I would claim coyly that I just wanted to see the color, and when she said it was turquoise, I pleaded, "But let me see," and she showed me, and I said something pedantic, Bob Rossian like, "That's not turquoise, that's teal," and then she'd begrudgingly show me again, and we had a debate about color all for an excuse to look down her shorts for longer. Once, I was nervy enough to reach into that shadow, to touch the mesh of her thong, even let my index finger slip between the elastic and stubble of her pelvis. There was a quiet click when the thong snapped back against the skin. I suspected she would let me put my fingers inside of her eventually. I hated that I was reminded of the episode of Doubting Thomas, needing to touch the hole to believe its existence. Until then, I had patient hormone-stricken thoughts about her.

Of course, though, Pearl eventually heard the story too. Our foreplay discontinued. One week, I was playing the panty palette game with her; the next, she refused to let me even kiss her.

"Not for a couple weeks," she said.

She had some elaborate theory about dog penises and germs, and she wanted to make sure I had brushed it all out of my mouth. I washed my mouth with Listerine hourly after school for weeks. Even now, when I use mouthwash, I think of Grizz, imagine I'm spitting out late generations of his germ. Before Pearl's prohibition had passed, though, she had been unfairly integrated into the myth (somebody had added that she liked to *watch* me suck my dog's dick), and she didn't want to see me ever again.

After Pearl broke up with me, I inspected her wallet-sized soccer picture, read the irony across her shirt: *Norwin Pride*. Without telling them why, I had already signaled my subtle approval as my parents considered an out-of-district move. They claimed they didn't want to uproot me, but I wanted nothing more than to move outside of the mythic borders. I knew that in the case of Dogsucker, displacement was the quickest evasion. The true antidote, though, was stowed in the genome of the myth.

In preparing to enter public high school, I conducted shaky legal web searches, but I couldn't decipher the myriad laws as they might relate to my case—of rape, assault, and involuntary deviate sexual intercourse. If the complainant was given the choice, for instance—to suck or not to suck—and he went for it (albeit to save a beloved pet), then it isn't exactly involuntary. Would the judge be a Virgil or an Ovid? Shout *A! Uirgo* at my prosecution or hide the gavel for fear I'd deep-throat it? Not to mention, there is the troublesome Title 18, Section 3129 from the Statutes of Pennsylvania, which states a person who engages in any form of sexual intercourse with an animal commits a misdemeanor of the second degree. I feared the prospect of juvenile hall.

Is it rape when your aggressor is giving you the option between a) taking indirect responsibility for the murder of a living thing, a best-ever present, or b) taking a penis in your mouth? Do conditions turn rape consensual? Or, is the question about rape moot because the penis belongs to a dog, and bestiality is the primary infraction? Did the fact of both parties being minors blur all legal consequence?

In my last months of Catholic school education, we read selections from Thomas Aquinas's *Summa Theologica*. I had been looking forward to reading it because I had carefully selected Thomas as my patron saint and adopted his name in the Sacrament of Confirmation. In his reply to objection number four,

Aquinas states that the "gravity of a sin depends more on the abuse of a thing than on the omission of the right use... the most grievous is the sin of bestiality, because the due species is not observed." In my last confession at Queen of Angels, I told Monsignor about how I masturbated, swore, lied to my parents, lusted after Vic (in church no less), lusted after Dani too, how I looked down her shirt when she leaned. And I told Monsignor there was something to which I wasn't ready to confess, so could I instead just confess to my withholding? Monsignor was not happy and called the confession incomplete. He quoted a biblical verse about cowardice, but doled his penance anyway.

The summer before high school, my public school friends told me not to be nervous about the transition, that everyone already knew me. They didn't understand that in the two years since the act, the story had evolved like untamed kudzu, that it was a creation story, and my anxiety was that I wasn't even present for my own genesis—the automythographer utterly absent. My pending 1600 high school peers only knew the myth of me. I had infamy and celebrity. I had enigma. I would if I could have retreated into anonymity, obscurity, but instead I was screwed by malignant myth. I was prudent in the last weeks of summer, refused to sing along while my friends played Nine Inch Nails' "Closer" ("I want to fuck you like an animal") and Bloodhoundgang's "Bad Touch" ("You and me baby ain't nothing but mammals / so let's do it like they do on the Discovery Channel"). Good fun turned bad.

I tried in earnest to convince my parents to send me to Pittsburgh Central Catholic High School, a long but worthwhile commute. *Look at the postgraduate Ivy placement*, for instance.

During my first "A Lunch" at Norwin High, in a cafeteria with 650 others, a group of boys, generic enough, approached my table and offered me ranch for my fries. I thanked them for the random kindness. After they left, I read the Sharpied container lid: *Grizz Jizz*. Later in the week, the same coterie caroled "This Old Man" behind me in the lunch line, emphasis on the "give a dog a bone" lyric. I tried shrugging it off, even joined

22

them in a failed harmonic round.

Others called me Dogsucker in the corridors and locker rooms and classrooms and principals' offices and bathrooms of Norwin High. They called me Dogsucker in the bleachers and under the bleachers and by the concessions stands of stadiums and on curbsides near guardrails during fire drills and in stairwells against the tiled walls.

They called me "Doggy Style" too; some thought it was cleverer than Dogsucker. In psychological epistemology, the primacy effect dictates that your first memory of something will serve as an eternal, privileged model no matter the recency effect of later phenomena. Even now, twelve years later, when my girlfriend asks if I want to switch to "doggy style"—a proposition that should make me want to high-five my erection—I cringe before acquiescing. And as I thrust, the pleasure conflicts me; the *crème de la crème* of sexual positions nearly renders me flaccid. "Doggy Style" didn't have the longevity of Dogsucker, though, because it was eventually abbreviated into "Doggy," then "Dawg," benign because I shared it with the same "wiggers" and "hicks" (so-called) that persecuted me.

I taped pieces of paper on the inside of my locker and numbered the lines. By the end of my freshman year, there were 72 names on the list. Each person on the list had either punched me in the jaw or the chin or the nose, kicked me in the crotch, contorted me into a field house locker, thrown me down the twenty-two steps from the swimming pool, picked me up and slammed me on concrete at the Circleville Fireman's Fair, given me the middle finger while spitting a chewing tobacco loogie at my face during a fire drill, batted my cheek with a psychology textbook, shot me with paintballs from a pavilion as I ran through Oak Hollow Park, showed me a knife ("Come here, let me show you something, fag.") and held it so close to my face that my eyelashes blinked against the blade, slammed my teeth into the water fountain spout while I was drinking and left me tooth-chipped and gum-bleeding through chemistry class, tripped me while I carried my chromosome project, took a lunch-line lunge at me for looking too long and sucker punched me in the gut, etc. When an observant hallway monitor told the principal about my list, Principal Nist summoned me. I had endured the ambiguous embarrassment of his office several times before, but had managed to keep my story encrypted. He thought the rolodex in my locker was some kind of Columbine hit list. He told me the next step could be a meeting with local police in the conference room. I assured him that I was not pre-meditating violent revenge.

In homeroom, I sat in solidarity with the punks while all the others stood and pledged the flag. A girl, Gianni, leaned toward me.

She said, "I don't talk to flags either."

Even though the defiance was aimless, it felt good to have a little control before the day's melee. After school, I smoked pot with new friends. Eventually, I was installed as a guitarist in a punk band, tried methamphetamines, cocaine, even PCP. This outcast cliché was a much-needed stability.

After one especially violent cafeteria fight (with Rushner no less), I was asked to explain to Dr. Nist how I got the nickname Dogsucker and why it became the viral cafeteria rally chant following my toppling of the uncoordinated Juggalo. Dr. Nist was candid in his perplexity, but there was something slightly unprofessional in the way he prodded. I explained it to him, a wrought synopsis. It made sudden sense to him, the reason I kept ending up in his office. I wasn't the antagonist; my myth was. It was a myth that provoked homophobic tirades from the children of conservative-minded Western Pennsylvania parents. Mercifully, Dr. Nist decided against calling my parents, and I returned to the dubious corridors of the high school labyrinth.

Bullfucker (continued): carmen et error

Behold the causality of myth. The labyrinth not just created for the sake of architectural conundrum, but constructed to house

24

the Minotaur. The Minotaur exiled not just because he was hideous and foul-tempered (allegedly, he was), but because he was the sire of bestial adultery and oracles recommended his imprisonment. Had Minos just swallowed his pride, stepped in as step-father to the chimera half-man half-bull, the Minotaur might have been a well-adjusted little boy-bull.

Before there was Virgil or Ovid, there was Euripides. In 400 B.C., Euripides stated in *Cretans* that a woman who commits adultery with a man is a sinner while sex with a bull can only be "divinely-inspired madness." Ovid's *Ars Amatoria* was a departure from the popular Gigantomachy genre in which the giants revenged the Olympian deities of the Greek Pantheon. Because he wrote in elegiac form—a poet speaking about the mores of his society—it became an exercise in applied mythology. It was Ovid's don't-say-I-didn't-tell-you-so to Roman men everywhere.

It turns out that the Romans weren't ready for Ovid's mythico-historical paradigmatic shift, though. In his final and unfinished work, *Exile*, he talks about why he was exiled from Rome: *Carmen et error.* 'Two charges, a poem and an error' ruined him. While the latter refers to an impudent affair Ovid had with Augustus Caesar's daughter, Julia, the poem is *Ars Amatoria*, which was too provocative, too progressive. Rather than invite his reader to peak into the usual telescope aimed at the overplayed gods, Ovid's revolutionary burlesque satire acted as a premature microscope on human relations. This reorientation caused his readers whiplash and his reputation backlash.

As for Pasiphaë, who may have otherwise been forgotten in weaker manifestations of her myth, her wretched existence in *Ars Amatoria* may at least be retroactively redeemed vis-á-vis the reassessment of feminist scholars such as Rebecca Armstrong.

Bullfucker (continued): post-Ovid

I've been spinning post-Ovidian myths in my dreams.
    ...in which Daedalus builds the hollow heifer, sure, but he

25

also castrates the snow-white bull because, in his capacity as genius, he foresees the Minotaur sire as evidence of zoophilia. In sterilizing the bull, he protects Minos from fury, Pasiphaë from shame, even Ovid from exile.

…in which Minos, in an act of love and reconciliation, anticipating Poseidon's *deus ex machina*, has Daedelus craft an impenetrable contraceptive, an ironclad chastity belt for his queen—rendering the bull impotent—at least until Pasiphaë's lust wears off.

…in which Athena, Poseidon's rival and saboteur, has her owl peck out the bull's eyes, and the bull roams wildly all around the proxy heifer, but never mounts, and Pasiphaë, growing impatient, returns home and fellates Minos.

…in which all remaining translations of *Ars Amatoria* on rust-manged gunmetal gray university shelves undergo rapid disintegration, a mythoptosis. The lignin breaks down into stinking acids. The pages turn brittle. In which the written record has faithfully replaced the oral, and I kick in my sleep because myth *is* material despite what I thought. In which information cryonics (whether by digitization or magnesium oxide preservatives) hasn't been able to keep up. In which all myths have been mortalized by cellulose decay, and Pasiphaë's story is alive only in the fetid funk of groundwood pulp.

…in which Pasiphaë—her wretched spirit—manifests two millennia later, and she is reincarnated in my myth. In which we somehow, by senior year, manage to defeat what seemed like an insurmountable stigma. In which we are somehow voted to Senior Homecoming Court as if we're vying for king like Minos before the bull came to shore. We are an underdog waiting to claim the throne to the high school. In which we walk to the fifty-yard line before thousands of people, and our name is echoing in the valley, our real name—not Bullfucker, not Dogsucker as everyone knew us in plastic prehistory—and we consider the box of ballots, our name written over and over again on tiny flags of white paper, certainly more submissions than were on the locker door's "hit list," and all because we found the antidote, our circle-circle-dot-dot. All because we became the master artificers of our own mythography, constructed ourselves narrative portals through which we could enter, participate, redact.

etc.

Dogsucker (continued): on tense

What if my parents had instead given me batteries on Christmas 1999? "For your Tamagotchi," they might have said. Or, what if Grizz had instead been a female dog, eradicating the anatomical possibility of my eponym.

In high school, my girlfriend Amanda provided steadfast defense. She refused to let anyone tell the unabridged version of my story. "Larry sucked his dog's dick" was never enough. "Yeah, because Rushner made him do it," she would append. I call her now, ask her to tell it to me as she remembers it.

"What do you mean? You walked Grizz to the bus stop. Then, Rushner got off the bus and took the leash. And he dragged Grizz across the road. Right? And then, he like, convinced you to like, well he told you he'd give the leash back if you sucked its dick." She whispers the last part.

"And then?" I ask.

"Why are you being weird about this? You know what then. You sucked his dick."

Amanda tells the story in simple past tense. *Walked, dragged, convinced, sucked.* These regular verb forms end with *–ed* to narrate events that are chronologically past. There is something inherited and removed about the authority. Something secondhand.

Amanda tells me that she saw Rushner at a house party a few months ago, that he was sitting on a porch step, drinking a Monster energy drink. In this I-still-got-your-back tone, she promises that she acted badly toward him. When he asked her why she was being such a bitch, she reminded him that she used to date me. "Remember? You made him suck his dog's dick?" she said to him.

I gasp. "*Seriously*? You said that? What did he say?"

The thing is, to my knowledge, nobody has ever—in the twelve years since the act—said anything like this to Rushner. It seems—if people really believed the story—Rushner's role was equally heinous. Shouldn't he have received some of the flak?

"He said he was doing you a favor letting you suck his dick because you're a faggot anyway."

So, Rushner was proud of his complicity.

When I call Jaybo, though—he was there, at the bus stop—the facts' tense transmogrifies.

Q: Were you there the day I sucked my dog's dick?

A: Yes.

Q: Where was Rushner?

A: He was still on the bus because his stop wasn't until Charles.

Q: He never got off?

A: No.

Q: How did it happen?

A: You were just being really weird. I don't remember why. We got off the bus, and you were sucking it for whatever reason. For like a second.

Q: And afterward?

A: We were playing basketball in my driveway.

The past progressive tense, also known as past continuous, has an eye witness quality to it. *Rushner was sitting. You were sucking. We were playing.* Each is formed with the past tense of be (*was/were*) followed by a present participle of the main verb. The past progressive indicates an action that was ongoing at the past time being considered.

A secondhand narrator like Amanda is virtually disallowed from using past progressive tense. It seems inherent to secondhand narration that the speaker's experience of the action was always past—always *–ed*—and so the perspective feels secondhand. An eye-witness or primary observer like Jaybo, however, has the capacity to narrate in either simple past or past progressive tense. Inherent to the past progressive is that habitual *–ing.*

The speaker, as he tells it, was present at the moment of the action being discussed, and he is still psychologically present in that moment when recounting, the memory so crystalline that he can't relegate it to the *–ed*.

Dogsucker (continued)

I finally go back to Pittsburgh, this dozen-year anniversary. I stand outside in blustery cold winds, pumping gas into my dad's Corvette. Both Amanda and Jaybo told me that Rushner was the cashier at the BP on Brownstown Road. Alongside a *You must be 18* tobacco sign, I see his chubby face in the window. The gas pump trigger is locked as the fuel gushes into the tank. I blow on my hands for warmth. I consider going in, consider buying holiday lottery ticket gifts here so that I can ask him: "No bullshit, Rushner. Just tell me: Were you even there the day I sucked my dog's dick? Were you there? How did it happen?" I am working up the courage as the pump trigger clicks. How do you even ask someone, "Did you or did you not make me…?"

Why set a record straight when the status quo has been to my advantage for so long? Why risk amnesia of his potentially false memory?

I look at Rushner through the gas station window. He is utterly unaware of my existence. I want to tap on the glass, stare at each other as if at a carnival mirror. In high school, Rushner threw a rock through my window. My dad swept the glass as I picked two river rocks off the carpet. In response, that same winter, I carved a gash in the aluminum of his above-ground pool so that it slow-leaked during the late February thaw. If I purchase the lottery tickets here, will the ensuing small talk bury or sharpen the hatchet? I hedge bets and buy the tickets at the Sunoco down the road. I've looked many times, but haven't found Monsignor's Bible verse on cowardice. Maybe he made it up.

If Jaybo's story is true, then what's in it for Rushner to insert himself into my fiction? The symbiosis of this myth, I suppose, relates to power. Perhaps I needed to appear powerless in order to save face with my middle school girlfriend, Pearl, and fearing eternal virginity, I made up a story that could elicit enough sympathy to ensure my act was counterbalanced. An emergency myth. Rushner, on the other hand, needed to appear power*ful*. He didn't reject his role because it advanced his brand, achieved for him new levels of desired infamy. It is a myth as myriad as the Greco-Roman vein, as literally oral as it gets. Perhaps Rushner's history of sadism is so rich that my invention of forced zoophilic rape on a minor is negligible. Or, he is so impressionable—his memory so plastic—that he can absorb any convenient fallacy I concoct. When I do encounter him again—when that courage occurs to me—I wonder if he'll issue an obtuse false apology or an acute pledge of gratitude.

On my last evening in Pittsburgh, I decide to ask Thom too. A tiebreaker perhaps.

L: Were you there the day I sucked my dog's dick?

T: Yes.

L: Was Rushner there?

T: Yes.

L: How did it happen?

T: I just remember Rushner's fat ass running down the street and thinking, 'I didn't know he could run that fast.'

L: How far did he run?

T: I don't know, like, the Derroch's? The Perry's?

L: It was the Tersey's.

T: Oh shit.

Q: Do you remember what we did afterward?

A: We probably played basketball in Jaybo's driveway.

Dogsucker (continued)

In my last memory of Grizz, I sat on the steel guardrail and waited for my father to pick me up from track practice at Norwin High School. I was with a dozen or more of my teammates. Mac, a member of the B-relay team, attached the gold-flaked relay baton to his crotch and stroked it with his eyes comically closed, mouth agape. There was mild laughter and some blank stares.

When my father pulled up to the curb in his blue Corvette, he put the passenger window down. Grizz, just six pounds, pawed his way up to the window's ledge. I held my breath as everyone hushed—even Mac whose baton dick went limp against his thigh. Everyone looked at Grizz, mascot of my myth. Grizz, who was used to many eyes upon him, seemed disquieted by all the fraught attention. It was as if they were, for the first time, meeting the *iuuencus*, sprung from myth to actuality. I opened the door and dropped into the bucket seat of the Corvette. Grizz took his position on my lap, paws back up to the window ledge, and I heard my teammates giddy with laughter under the engine's rev. I yanked at Grizz's leash, doing my best to make him invisible. Make him go away.

As my father pulled away, I neglected to wave goodbye to anyone. In the rearview, Mac pretended to fellate the baton, his tongue pushing at the inside of his cheek. From twenty yards away at the first stop sign, I could hear the energized response to Mac's lewd pantomiming. I put the window up.

"Can you not bring Grizz with you when you pick me up anymore?" I asked.

Bewildered, my father agreed, pulling at the leash until Grizz was on *his* lap.

I return to Tucson tomorrow. I am getting restless in the old neighborhood. Inside my parent's house, I watch television and occasionally peek at the mantel where they keep a lifelike statue of a Yorkshire Terrier that wears Grizz's actual collar. In my every memory of Grizz, he is substituted by this statue now: in the Pet Taxi on Christmas Eve; in the Garasy's driveway; in the Corvette in the garage; he is especially a statue in the memory in which he slipped beneath the neighbor's fence, where one of two retired racing dogs—greyhounds who once

31

chased mechanical, Yorkie-sized rabbits—snapped Grizz's neck out of natural instinct and killed him.

The statue has no genitalia as if it was part of Pope Pius XII's iconoclastic castration of Roman sculptures. The sight of animal genitalia—even ceramic cock and balls—can provoke an anxiety within me so profound that it regularly occurs to me to just lust after these animals, to perform a self-conscious self-fulfilling prophecy. I have dog-sat for friends and for professors and have been paralyzed by irrational guilt when the crotch-nuzzling dog comes near. When a woman at Himmel Park tells me, "Go ahead, you can pet my dog," I hesitate. I feel like I should confess to my stigma rather than pose a threat to her Lhasa Apso. When I'm convinced the Yorkie statue is looking at me, I turn off the television and avert my eyes.

In the backyard, I fill the birdfeeders with seed. Winter cardinal, winter jay, winter titmouse feast here. I accidentally spill the bag onto the ground and rake the spillover of seeds, chips, and kernels across hard sallow yard. I am raking and shivering just a couple feet above where Grizz is buried.

Until now, the only written version of this story that existed—the hasty urtext—was that which Dr. Nist scribed as part of my school record, and then shredded upon graduation. I know I am resuscitating a myth that has otherwise grown mute, its oscillations diminished and absorbed into unexceptional suburban static. It may be that I write out of deference to my deranged creation lore; it may be too that I am pleading again for a dog, that this is my mythic taxidermy of his corpus.

The Well-Stocked and Gilded Cage: *Psittaculture Nervosa*

1 | The morning after the quake (magnitude 6.0), my first since moving to California, I call my mother, happy to break a cycle of redundant conversations about DMV, home owner's insurance, and what percentage moved in we are. As she gauges the completeness of our move-in ("I don't know, seventy-five percent, should be closer to eighty tomorrow," I say stupid things like this), I can tell she is actually gauging abstract phenomena like dishonesty (hadn't I promised a homecoming?) and guilt (have I any?).

"It sounded like luggage wheels on a wooden floor," I tell her. "Actually, it *felt* like luggage wheels. If that makes sense." Her response is lackluster, not as I imagined it would be. Just a few follow-up questions about aftershocks and *How far is Napa again?* as the crow flies and as it doesn't.

"Your cousin had another seizure last night," my mother says. It is her fifth this month. The doctors are still deciding on dosages. I ask my mother about the magnitude of this recent seizure, but she says she doesn't think that's how seizures work. I know I am conflating earthquake and epilepsy, Richter pen and electrode, fault line and scalp. I am hopelessly essaying. We hang up. I spend the day unpacking.

At night, my girlfriend sleeps, and I roam through the new house, learning which boards squeak, which neighbors stay up late, which neighbors work late (i.e., deal drugs). I shave so quietly that between drags of the razor, I hear my own breath solo for the first time in months. I decide that I wear ear buds too often. I dry my hands on my girlfriend's nightgown because it's hanging on a towel hook. I eat baby carrots, chew softly. I read articles about Syria, celebutantes, and *gaegogi* (dog meat), wondering if my cousin is having another seizure now or maybe now. I read articles about seizures.

Then Arni, small and blue, my parrotlet (see "pocket parrot"), drops from his perch, flaps, and transforms into a strident alarm system, a bleating echo. My girlfriend wakes. We meet at the cage. She asks what is wrong with him, and what's wrong with me, why am I up so late. She holds the kitten we've just adopted, a small tuxedo like Sylvester. I tell her Arni has only had a night terror once before. I don't know what's wrong.

She goes back to sleep, and I rotate Arni in my palm as if inspecting a feathered pinecone. I check his eyes for dilation, his wing for broken blood feathers. I roll away a small pin feather and feel his heart beat like a neuron caught between pinball bumpers. From the way he shrugs, I can tell his carpal joint is wounded. I start asking him questions, only some spoken aloud.

"What's wrong Arni?
Did you feel an aftershock?
What is this place, buddy?
Huh?
What woke you up?
What caused your fright?
Did you hurt yourself?
Are you hurt?
Do you miss Arizona?
Do you miss the desert?
Do you, mister?
You haven't adjusted yet, have you?
Is it the moths?
Is it the cat?"

After he settles into his hammock, sleeping with head revolved and eyes open, I insert ear buds and watch YouTube in the dark, an early episode of *Canary Row*, Tweety singing á la voice actor Mel Blanc's affectation of a precious speech impediment: "I'm a tweet wittow biwd in a gilded cage; tweety'th my name but I don't know my age. I don't have to wuwy and dat is dat; I'm tafe in hewer from dat ol' putty tat."

2 | Arni can gulp, kiss, scuff, bounce, trickle, sneeze, cough, and belch. He can replicate most iPhone sounds (e.g., apex, beacon, bulletin, chimes, cosmic, crystals, presto, radar, etc.). I've taught Arni words too, but he's mostly apathetic about lingual mimicry.

Whereas human speech is achieved through phonation, the effect of vocal folds (see "vocal cords") vibrating hundreds of times per second within the larynx (see "voice box"), bird song is achieved through a small organ unique to birds, the syrinx. Because of the syrinx, birdsong is composed almost purely of air (compare with humans: just 2 percent air), meaning Arni's voice is more like an enunciative whistle than it is my own.

The syrinx, which has been compared to a double-reeded oboe or French horn in its construction, derives its name from the Grecian nymph Syrinx. In Thomas Woolner's *Silenus* (1884), Syrinx's story is adapted into an erotic narrative poem: "Syrinx [is] chased by nimble Pan"—Pan the satyr, god of wild—"flushed with terror, plucked at by demon claws, [she] plunges"—(see "Pan-ic")—"in the stream and her young spirit passes into the reeds." Pan proceeds to cut the reeds at different lengths, fashions pipes (see "pan flute"), and his hostile breath generates a necrophilic song.

In their publication "How Do Birds Sing?" researchers Stephen Nowicki and Peter Marler explain that before the sonagraph, researchers had to "annotate birdsong on musical staff," using Western musical notation such as the crotchet (♩) (see Arni's "salutation") and quaver (♪) (his "excitable") and semiquaver (♫) ("territorial") and demisemiquaver (for "preemptive attack") and hemidemisemiquaver (for "night terror").

The morning after the night terror, Arni perches on my shoulder, and Bing Crosby revolves on the phonograph. When Bing Crosby, Harry Belafonte, Leonard Cohen, or Matt Berninger sing a C2 at 65 Hz, Arni sporadically accompanies with a C7 (2093 Hz), an interval duet. Larynx and syrinx. When Joan Baez sings, Arni'll cock his head and trill along. Larynx and syrinx. When I say his name, he sometimes parrots back, "Arni!" Larynx and syrinx. If Arni goes too long without larynx, though, he weeps, a natural (see "unlearned") crying sound effect. He only makes the sound when he's alone. Syrinx. Syrinx. Syrinx. Syrinx.

In Woolner's poem, Syrinx's lover, the eponymous Silenus, stays beside the river and "the reeds before him sigh… [and] every tongue tells something to the breeze." Silenus remarks that Syrinx is a "frail debtor to the wind for voice to tell [her] dark sorrowing." I watch Arni as if he is a feathered reed, a flaccid windsock.

3 | My bird, as bewildered as you are in the new house—you've your own corner with crown molding, a cage twice as big, white vinyl ropes intersecting like Escher stairs, forming many angular letters (i.e., I, K, L, M, N, T, V, W, Y, and Z), by which to play at anagrams of your possible paths (e.g., vim, zit, wilt, kiln, etc.), a wooden swing and fibrous circus rings, a three-piece triangular vanity mirror, two pine perches, a calcium perch, cuttlebone, a washcloth hammock with clothespin clamps, millet spray and deep seed dishes, a bowl for sipping and another for bathing, freely defecating from wherever because gravity plumbs universally to a sewer of fresh newspaper—you're pretty hooked up, aren't you? *Aren't* you?

Bewilder, from be- + archaic *wilder*, what lures you into the wilds now, in this, our most domestic predicament to date? I see your brown eyes widened, your tiny lashes quivered, hear your whim-

pers when I work in another room. I hear you cry, and joblessness makes me want to do the same. What if I let you just grow
them out and fly away? This coop need be flown by either one
of us. Let's sit on the porch, flirt with the perimeter of the domicile, contemplate departures.

4 | With clean powder blue silk cloth boards (a little sunned),
blind stamped decoration, unchipped gold lettering on cover
and spine, minimally bumped and edgeworn, small tears on the
headcap and tail, water damage to joints, loose binding, and
clean pages (with exceptions of free end pages and pp. 31-32),
Notes on Cage Birds., collected and edited by Dr. W. T. Greene
in 1882, my only "antique book," looks just like you.

I handle it just the same, lifting it from the reclining iron book-
stand, the only forward-facing book in the house. I catch you
rotating on its cover when I refill my coffee mug, blue-on-blue
spinning on blue. Remember Zenk, the ROTC roommate who
checked in on you when I went to Akron some weekends? He
found it at a giant book auction in Archer City, Texas.

5 | It is easy to immobilize you. It takes just three fingers to

delay your flight. I curl them around your breast, abdomen, and flanks, and with your permission, lift a wing with my thumb. The other hand, the one I've been hiding at my side, has got fingers already through the scissor's eye rings. I coax your flight feathers, cascade them open, see the gradient of the cobalt coverts to your turquoise flight feathers. They say you've got at least sixty-five feathers on each wing, though I've never actually counted. Some are just too small.

When I restrain you, curl you tighter against my palm and fix your feathers so they're wholly fanned, you hook your bill into my flesh as if splitting a seed. A bead of blood trickles down my knuckle as I trim your feathers. No hard feelings. Of the sixty-five alleged, only twenty are "flight feathers." Of those, I clip just five (primaries six through ten). When you wriggle, I feel your heartbeat accelerate. Your wings tremble. These vibrations within you syncopate against my palm. You feel like an instrument, a feathered maraca or egg shaker. I try out a pun because it feels like a gentle thing to do. "Lookin' fly, Arni." It only serves to ease my own anxiety about clipping your feathers.

How to Trim Primary Flight Feathers 6-10 (Viewed from Above)

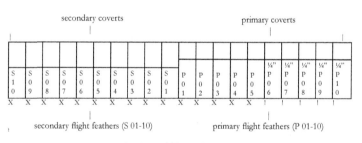

secondary coverts										primary coverts									
															¼"	¼"	¼"	¼"	¼"
S 1 0	S 0 9	S 0 8	S 0 7	S 0 6	S 0 5	S 0 4	S 0 3	S 0 2	S 0 1	P 0 1	P 0 2	P 0 3	P 0 4	P 0 5	P 0 6	P 0 7	P 0 8	P 0 9	P 1 0
X	X	X	X	X	X	X	X	X	X	X	X	X	X	X	!	!	!	!	!

secondary flight feathers (S 01-10)   primary flight feathers (P 01-10)

key: ! = cut ¹/₂" X = do not cut

I repeat the ordeal on the other side so that they'll grow in evenly, so that your aerodynamism is balanced. Your first post-trim flight is a parabola destined for the floor. You look disoriented, as if you've just discovered that flying is not just like riding a bike after all. Not with my cruel intervention. I scoop you up and set you on a platform in your cage. You survey the new house as no-fly zone, try takeoff once more, but still parabolic—not flying, but falling as I would. I want to cite the time you flew into a pot of boiling water, the time you flew atop the ferret cage, the time you flew across the yard. I want to instill in you the dangers of flight, but it feels asinine because you were born with feathers, and I was born with scissors.

6 | Arni's breakdown has driven me to pry *Notes on Cage Birds* delicately open. It's the first time I've actually sat with the book since it was gifted to me Christmases ago. I scout for evergreen wisdom—some archaic phrasing on the management of cage birds—that has been muted in contemporary sources like *The Parrotlet Handbook* or Birdchannel.com. From the index, I pursue the following passages:

Insomnious, the page-turning turns reckless by 2:50 a.m. The brittle pages crinkle and chip. I am increasingly unnerved by the collective voice of these British writers. Chapter two opens with a quotation from "Natural History of Room or Chamber Birds" (1794): "Birds beings very tender creatures, on passing from a state of liberty to one of slavery, in which they lose the means of exercise and proper food, are soon afflicted with many diseases occasioned by this change alone" (32). Written thirty-nine years before the passage of the Slavery Abolition Act of 1833, this "venerable father of Cage Bird Lore" doesn't mince words.

Other pages (i.e., 20 & 107) refer to caged birds as inmates, a fair term since the principal function of the cage is to confine. A melee of commercial modifiers has softened the fact of "cage" in this century: designer cage, deluxe cage, signature series cage, protégé cage, Victorian cage, ranch style cage, Silverado cage, tree top cage, clear view cage, and cage with jumbo tiel scrollwork. FeatherStone Heights' line of cages doesn't sell cages at all, but Cape Cods, Stone Cottages, Brownstones, and Tudors. Of course, the cheapie façades fail to disguise what is, in essence, a fairly standard cage design.

In stocking Arni's cage, I realize I am probably just furnishing his prison. I remember peering into Al Capone's lavish cell while on a tour of Philadelphia's Eastern State Penitentiary—its oriental rugs, imported furniture, the warm lamp, and cabinet radio. Somebody in my group said "World's luckiest inmate" under his breath, and that notion throbbed in my head for the duration of the tour.

At night, the perches and toys and bowls within the cage appear as a flotilla. Sleepiness or scotch diminishes my depth perception, and the bars of the cage seem to disappear. Because his eyes are on the side of his head, Arni does this funky head bob to achieve motion parallax, to get a relative sense of the proximity of objects in the world outside of his cage. I think about how most of any day, Arni is forced to perceive through quarter-inch gaps between two hundred and twelve iron bars. "Sleep well, tonight, little man," I tell him, leaning in. "As you were."

7 | As caged as you have been most of your life, remember Pittsburgh, where I removed the blinds for you, zip-tied twelve feet of Jo-Ann Fabric leafy vines from the window frame brackets, and they bowed across the room. You'd shimmy left or right for views of vestigial smokestacks from Pittsburgh's industrial past, discharging romantic puffs on the horizon like artificial climate. I installed more and more vines in the bedroom, from the bronze scalloped cage to the bookshelf, from the cage to the loft bed rails.

On walks home from campus libraries or laboratories, I scouted for fallen branches, forked and sapless. I'd sit on the stoop and amputate meristems, shear leaves, and soak the branches in buckets of water with bleach to kill off larvae. Rinse, dry, rinse again. Then, I'd take down my posters and maps, rolled and stored them in a closet, instead installing Lowe's brackets to the drywall, from which I secured the branches.

I forfeited my space to you, square foot by square foot, until it was a makeshift forest canopy with a human mattress somewhere within, as natural as the exhibits at The National Aviary in the North Side, where I went on Sundays to imagine further renovations of your wild. When I left you for a couple hours, NPR kept good company, but if I was on a whole-day ditch, I'd shuffle the "Birdchat" playlist, a compilation of ten hours of bird songs, parrot mimicry, audio recordings of my voice, of your voice, and the occasional song about a bird.

Once, I came home late, and any one of the sixteen sound spectrograms of the wren played at ½ or ¼ speed (I could never tell the difference), and it took me a long time to find you. I stalked the room, ducking at branches, tip-toeing or crouching at your favorite perches, endured the harrowing spectrum of avian bioacoustics on Bose surround sound: three-wattled bellbird, Tennessee warbler, and nuthatch. I worried you had somehow escaped. I began looking for holes in the ground, holes in the wall, open window gaps. I was scrambling through a frenzied and familiar landscape (I have recurring nightmares of pet owner errors-turned-terrors) until I found you, half-sleeping, camouflaged on a branch extending behind the bookshelf, a branch I could not remember placing there, and you were halfway to the pillow on my loft bed. I simply whispered "goodnight" to you as Leonard Cohen grumbled "Bird on the Wire." Thems were the wilds, Arni, I know, two bachelors in their pad-as-nest.

8 | Years ago, I would drive to Rector on irregular weekends, a small town in Pennsylvania's large Appalachian Plateau Province. Along Powdermill Run Road, my SUV passed roadside nets clotted with caught wild birds: ruby-throated hummingbirds, white-throated sparrows, Tennessee warblers, catbirds,

brown thrashers. I'd park by a white brick building, and inside, a scruffy red-eyed man was waiting for me with coffee. Along the inside wall, a clothesline shimmered with dozens of colorful carabiners hooked to the drawstrings of black, tan, and white sacks, which fidgeted and squawked. One by one, he would remove a bird from a sack, gave me a few seconds to shakily call out its species ("redpole—no redstart") and if I failed, he didn't hesitate to say it himself: "roughwing swallow."

He'd proceed to measure its wings with a small ruler, monitor molting patterns, blow the plumage to check for fat deposits, determine its sex and a rough age, drop it head first into a cup on a scale, and finally, with pliers, he'd fit a small band around its ankle. I recorded the data while sneaking glimpses of each bird, tracking less pertinent, less empirical data (i.e., bird as "content," "fearful," "anxious," "pissed off," "really pissed off," "panicky"). We'd stay in the banding station all morning while other volunteers with empty sacks trekked to Coot Slough, Plover Pool, Heron Pond, Alder Pond, Crisp Pond, to hedgerow gaps and marshy fields, willow and alder-lined streams, wherever mist nets were extended.

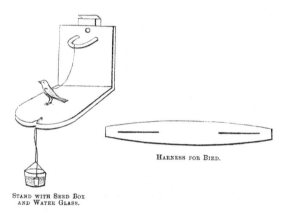

HARNESS FOR BIRD.

STAND WITH SEED BOX
AND WATER GLASS.

On any given morning at Powdermill Avian Research Center, I'd witness as many as seventy birds transition from wild to captive to wild again. The nets function like the green warp pipes in Super Mario Bros., a round-trip transport from one world to another. Some birds, paralyzed in their duress, looked at me with their giant eyes, a focus so intense it felt like one-sided telepathy. One re-recaptured American goldfinch—a recidivist, I joked then—held its beak hopelessly open, and instead of its usual *per-chicory*, a cheery undulating call, it glared at me while releasing a nasal teeee sound. I was impermeable to its message. In seconds, the conservationist handling her opened the station's trap door, and the finch flew free.

I'd walk the birds that were too big for the trap door, or especially rare species, to the road and release them on my own. Holding together the feet of a pileated woodpecker or a belted kingfisher, a mourning warbler or white-breasted nuthatch, or once, at a night banding session, a pair of Northern saw-whet owls (a pair of feet in each hand), I'd say something trite and encouraging like "good luck" or "don't be a stranger." As their digits launched from mine, a disoriented trajectory for the hedge or tree line, I thought of Arni, who was born in an unbeatable glitch level of Super Mario Bros., something like "Minus World," which traps the character indefinitely.

After a morning of banding, Arni sat in my palm, preening his clipped wings before the streaky windows. Did he know all that air could be his? I worried there were undercurrents of pining in his surveillance of the Carnegie smokestacks. "Release" was the one thing I could never do for him, but I've tried to compensate with all the others.

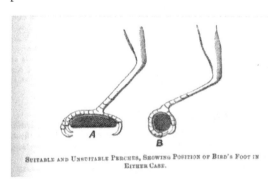

SUITABLE AND UNSUITABLE PERCHES, SHOWING POSITION OF BIRD'S FOOT IN EITHER CASE.

9 | My cousin's sixth seizure does not coincide with California quake or Arni night terror. She convulses until she doesn't. While my mother explains all the things the doctor does not yet know, I imagine Jessie collapsing and convulsing in various places throughout our hometown, and I get sad: in the dandelions at Indian Lake, at the salad bar at Eat n' Park, in front of the ice cream freezers at Kerber's Dairy. I imagine her collapsing at Café Down Under even though I don't think she's ever been there. I imagine her collapsing at sites that aren't even there anymore: Ye Olde Teddy Bear Shoppe (closed), our grandmother's house (rented), the deck of our uncle's pool (deconstructed).

As my mom talks, I start to feel guilty that I am not having seizures. I look at my hand, make it tremble like Parkinson's, imagine how awful to lose control. When I was a lifeguard, I removed a man from the ocean as he seized, put a towel around him as he voided his bowels. When I asked him if he knew where he was, he said, "The water. The water. Big bath."

When we hang up with mom, I remove Arni from the cage and take him to my hovel in the loft. He swivels his head so that I can itch each part of his neck.

10 | As caged as you have been most of your life, remember Pittsburgh, where I once ran late for a biology lecture, and rushing from my apartment into winter, the roads streaked with salt, Oakland Avenue all bundled up, everyone wearing galoshes and hats with pom-poms, and Arni, you were inexplicably there, though I didn't know it for a half mile. You had quietly flown into my hood before I left our room (I was probably wearing ear buds), and I walked you through the urban streets—past Primanti's, past Panera, past the Cathedral of Learning, past the bus stops on Forbes, past so many pacing pigeons—like a parrot palanquin, royalty conveyed, until a guy was pointing at me, and I yanked the ear buds as he said to his son, "Look, this dude's got his bird trained to ride in his hood." You were not trained as

such, but thank you anyway for not flying away.

11 | As blue as you are, not as blue as you have been. With your fingers wrapped around mine, digits cracked, nails sharp, I rotate you mid-air, *forpus coelestis*, an about-time inspection of the pocket parrot post-relocation. You occasionally itch at your neck, and a cloud of fine dust disseminates. The plumage of your breast and abdomen are powder blue while your wings, flight feathers, and tail feathers grade cobalt to turquoise. You know this already because you admire yourself most of the day in the tri-fold mirror. Your orange beak is paler now, a little chipped as to square off the hook bill. You choke, and I remove a gray feather from your tongue, roll it in my fingers, and flick it away.

The move has instigated a premature molt, so your hormones are in flux. You shed like a bough, your feathers to the floor, and the dirt cup of the vacuum looks like a violent plucking perch. Waxen cuticles emanate from your face, as yet unpreened. I twist the protein in my fingers, and your newest feathers open up.

But one thing's always the same: if you'll let me, I carefully separate the wings, exposing the one-inch-by-one-inch patch you conceal from all others. The silken feathers, contrasting starkly with the rest of your plumage, are a color Crayola could never recreate. I've searched for its name on color wheels, and decided that maybe it's mauveine. Mauveine, variously recorded as "Rosolan, Violet paste, Chrome violet, Anilin violet, Anilin purple, Perkins violet, Indisin, Phenamin, Purpurin, Tyralin, Tyrian purple, [and] Lydin" in Leffman and Beam's *Select Methods of Food Analysis* (1901), is your secret dimorphism. Except for rare acrobatic preening, even you are oblivious to the patch. It is the one part of you—regardless of cracked skin, sharp nails, pale beak, chipped beak, square beak, feathers falling, cuticles shooting—that is immutable.

12 | *Notes on Cage Birds.*, my copy, is supplemented with newspaper clippings—"Canaries Suffering with Asthma," "Insects in Cages, on Pets, Pigeons, &c.," "J.T.B.—Dead Parrot," "Canary Wheezy," "German Canary Losing Feathers," "Cleansing an Aviary," etc. A previous owner of this book—maybe E. F. Vibart (who inscribed his name on May 25, 1882)—carefully pasted these to the free end pages and over advertisements. He also threaded a small wood nail, now rusty, through page 118, affixing a folded piece of paper.

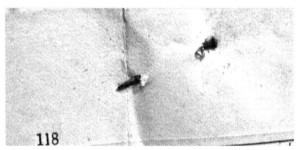

I remove the nail, smooth the punctures on the page, and unfold the attachment. Its impeccable cursive script details the inventory for J. Abrahams' fancier store. The script may belong to J. Abrahams himself.

Illiger's macaws (40/- each.)
Blue-fronted amazon parrots (from 35/- upwards)
Yellow-fronted amazon parrots (40/- each.)
Goffin's cockatoos, males & females, very same, £4 & £5 each.
Bare-eyed cockatoos, same, commencing to speak £5 each.
Rosebreasted cockatoos 15/- each.
1 pair same red-earred parrots, rare £4.-
Cockatiels 15/- pair.
Rosellas 20/- each.
sold. Pennan's parrakeets, in full colour, 30/- each.
Blue bonnet parakeets 30/- each.
Blue mountain lorikeets £3 pair.
Zavan parrakeets 25/- each.
Tirica parrakeets 20/- pair
White-eared conures 20/- pair
Golden-fronted conures 20/- pair
Cactus conures 20/- pair.
St. Thomas conures 30/- pair.
Ariel Toucans 25/- each.
Australian bronzewinged pigeons 50/- pair

Australian peaceful doves 30/-pair
Indian zebra doves 10/- pair
Masked Cape doves 25/- pair
Van Viennens land quails £2 pair.
3 Indian whistling ducks £5.-
2 Australian black swans £8.-
Cereopsis geese £8 pair
1 short-headed phalanger £2.-
Australian oppossums £2 each.
Marmozet monkeys £2 pair
Rhesus monkeys, same 35/- each
1 pair Emeus £30.-
Crimson-crested cardinals 15/- pair
Green, cardinals, only hens, 20/- each
African wattled starlings, 40/- pair
Parson Finches, * the pair
Whitish Javas
Address for letters: J. Abrahams, Naturalist, 191 & 192 St. George Street East,
London E. Registered telegraphic address: Abrahams Naturalist London. For
weekly arrivals, please, see "Land & Water."
P.T.O (please turn over)
Chinese mocking birds, males 40/-, females 30/- each.
Indian hill mynahs, large kind, 50/- each.
African simple bulbuls, very rare, 60/- pair
Persian white eared bulbuls 40/-pair
White-cheeked bullfinch larks, males 30/- each
Olivaceous saltahors 60/- each.
Superb tanagers in full colour, 50/- each
Scarlet tanagers " " " 50/- "
Violet tanagers " " " 40/- "
Crowned tanagers, male & female, 60/- pair
Paradise whydahs, not in colour 10/- pair, in colour 15/- pair, tail imperfection
Pin-tailed whydahs, " " " 10/- " in colour 15/- pair
Orange bishops " " " 10/- " " " 15/- "
Crimson-crowned bishops " " " 15/- " " " " 30/- "
Rufous necked weavers, males in colour 12/1. each.
Abyssinian weavers, " " " 20/. "
Red-billed and Russ' weavers 7/6 pair
Napoleon bishops 10/. Pair
Grenadier bishops 40/- pair
Yellow-backed bishops 40/- pair
Golden-fronted bishops 40/- pair.
Madagascar bishops, males 12/- each.
Saffron finches 12/6 pair
Zebra finches 7/6 pair
Cape sparrows, males 10/- each.
Yellow-throated sparrows 10/- pair
Zinca finches 30/- pair.
Fawn and white Japanese mannikins 15/- pair
Combassous 5/- pair.
Grey Javasparrows 5/- pair.
Striated mannikens 7/6 pair
Silverbills 5/- pair
Cutthroat finches 5/- pair
Grey wax bills 4/- pair
Grey singing finches 10/- pair
Terms: Cash with order.
All travelling cages charged extra.

Money for empties refunded, if returned in good condition and carriage free.
All goods are forwarded at consignee's risk and carriage forwarded.

The inventory incites my constant anxiety about pet ownership. It is reminiscent of my most recurrent nightmare, in
which I am managing a pet store, but failing. The store is dark
because light bulbs haven't been replaced. The fetor of feces
is absorbed in every air molecule. I am sprinting from cage to
tank to register. Mice are running loose, gnawing ankles. I have
birds perched the length of my arms, all squawking, some with
mutant attributes. The most horrifying is a beakless macaw; its
mouth is just an opening with a thick tongue. It eats the legs of
a tarantula, which writhes in pain on a bed of mulch. Fish float
dead in tanks. An electric eel has fractured the glass while trying to attack a rainbow-colored Mandarin goby in an adjacent
tank. Water leaks on a chameleon's head. Its eyes are recessed
in its skull. I look for tweezers. The eel generates an electric
shock, and a puffer fish expands, turns upside down. Seahorses
are neighing. I accidentally kick a tortoise on the ground, and its
shell falls off. It looks like a tiny dinosaur. I retreat to the stock-
room, hide among crickets and mealworms, stockaded by large
bags of birdseed, waiting for things to reset.

I search for "J. Abrahams naturalist importer" in web ar-
chives. Aside from full-page ads in various nineteenth-century
books for bird fanciers, Abrahams' name is mentioned in just
one other source, Donald Shaw's *London in the Sixties* (1908).
Shaw describes a treacherous section of London populated
by drunken sailors, unwashed women, "unsavoury tadpoles,"
inebriated foreigners, and rows of loafers "with a striking re-
semblance to the 'unemployed.'" "Not four years ago," Shaw
writes, "a respectable tradesman, Abrahams, a naturalist, of 191,
St. George's Street East, was attacked a [sic] 2 p.m., within fifty
yards of his own door, and succumbed to his injuries within
twenty-four hours."

I imagine J. Abrahams, the calm bird-keeper, standing
among the exact inventory as handwritten, folded, and nailed to

page thirty-one of *Notes on Cage Birds*; it's a ready-made snapshot of the scale of his establishment, an idyllic inverse of the pet store in my nightmare.

IF YOU WISH TO PURCHASE

FOREIGN BIRDS

OR

PET ANIMALS,

In his last minutes before the attack, he side-steps along rows of cages with containers of seed and pails of water, emptying them into dishes for the birds, speaking to the birds, whistling for the birds, the birds whistling back, hundreds of syrinxes, reeds of different sizes, piping like a transcontinental avichorus. His last action before leaving the store and locking its door is to inspect the crowned tanagers to see if they are nearing "full colour," only to be knifed in the girdle by sailors in sea-boots—then collapsing, spilling crimson.

Shaw assures his readers that decades later, the morality of St. George's Street had been revived by naturalist merchants who had taken Abrahams cue: "Now… rooms, once devoted to orgies [are] filled to their utmost capacity with canaries sending up songs to heaven… Continuing along St. George's Street will be found Jamrach's menagerie, whence filter most of the rarities that find their way to the Zoological Gardens…"

13 | I rotate the aluminum band clockwise around your leg, read your origins aloud: D-E-1-0-6-I-P-S-K-B-1. Counterclockwise, it's K-B-1-I-P-S-0-8-D-E. Do you know how much of your story is stored in this gram? You were born in Delaware in 2008, identified by your breeder (acronym KB1) as No. 106, and registered with the International Parrotlet Society. From this scant prologue, your biogeography dilates.

D E
0 8
1 0 6
IPS
K B 1

In DE, we made our first friends of a feather—the boardwalk gull colonies and duck rafts by lake. In PA, you played lush at jay parties and were swarmed by sparrow hosts on the backyard bough. In OH, a charm of goldfinches knew your mimicry to be flattery. In AZ, chimes of cactus wren craved your bowl of water as descents of woodpecker perched on saguaro, watching over you. The road trips between saw murmurations of starling, kettles of hawk, and murders of crow. As known as you have been most of your life, you will continue to be just so.

14 | The last newspaper clipping glued to the inside back board of *Notes on Cage Birds.* advises bird owners on how to send dead birds for postmortem examination to Dr. W. T. Greene, Peckham Rye, Surrey (and not to the office of the newspaper). The following rules are laid out for sending subjects for examination:

1. *Always send the bird off as soon as possible after death, otherwise a full examination cannot be guaranteed.*
2. *Always pack a dead bird in a tin or wooden box, never in cardboard, which is apt to be crushed in the post, and the inclosed destroyed or lost.*
3. *Always send a bird and the note respecting it in the same parcel, as it is not always possible to identify before or after the receipt of the birds themselves.*
4. *Always mention the variety of the bird sent, and state as fully as possible all particulars of age, treatment, duration of illness, &c., as, without such data, it is often impossible to answer the questions asked with accuracy.*

Dr. W. T. Greene must have received dozens of tin boxes, their enigma—much like the enigma of the black drawstring sacks at the Powdermill banding station—dissolved when the doors yawned open, revealing birds of varying species, dead, their bodies in different stages of decomposition. Many of the subjects were likely purchased at Abrahams' in East London since he advertised in Greene's books, or if not Abrahams', an establishment like his. What did Dr. Greene do with the birds after the postmortem examination—after, for instance deciding that a blood vessel had ruptured in the brain? Inter? Incinerate? Return to sender?

There is something uniquely somber about a dead bird. After a lifetime spent on its feet, a bird just capsizes. Years ago, I found my Gloster Canary, Peden, in repose at the bottom of his cage. I watched him, waited for a flinch or miraculous hiccup, but the dark feathers of his crown drooped like one of the Ramones. Wrapped in paper towels, I committed the bundle to an emptied box of wild sweet orange Tazo Tea, then committed the box to a brick-sized hole in the backyard of my parent's house.

Ignoring calls from home (three this hour), I watch you, Arni, still gripping at your suitable perch, still standing in your well-stocked and gilded cage. I am hoping life is at least better than could have been expected. I wish you would just say so. Syrinx. Just say "so."

Kumari Amenorrhea

I.

At 9 a.m., I stand in the courtyard of Kumari Ghar, blinking at the three windows where she, the new living goddess, is rumored to appear for a few seconds each day. The palace was built in the mid-18th century—one decade before the modern Kingdom of Nepal began—as expiation to the original Kumari after the last of the Malla Kings (probably) raped her. I study its wood relief and stone façade, disregarding its obvious signs of renovation in favor of the monastic whole.

A Hindu priest says to me, "I assure you that maybe she'll come after nine and before eleven." *I assure you… maybe.* I am well-trained in the art of dubious waiting: how many summer afternoons I'd spent in the queues of Sandusky, inching closer and closer to provisions of adrenaline from top-thrill coasters before the dreaded standstill: preventative maintenance detecting frayed cables, cracks in the welding, a dysfunctional chain dampener, gearbox, or sprocket.

I don't need the priest's assurances, though. I have a few hours to spare in Durbar Square anyway. Due to Kathmandu's load shedding schedule, there is a strategic blackout in the "backpacker ghetto" of Thamel through noon. Until then, the balmy streets clamor with "Just got back from base camp!" and "Next time, let's go to base camp!" and "Guided tours to base camp!" chatter. These palatial plazas are a respite from the acrophilic ennui.

Kumari is an attraction. Tourists clot and unclot in the courtyard of her *ghar*, which has been likened to a cage. A former Kumari, Samita Bajracharya, says she was only permitted to leave her house a dozen times a year for ceremonial functions. Because Kumari's feet are sacred, not allowed to touch the ground for her entire tenure, she is conveyed (at age eight,

53

nine, ten, eleven, and sometimes beyond that) in her parents' arms to her chariot or palanquin.

Even now, as the new Kumari settles into her monastic palace at Durbar Square, Western activists are trying to dismantle this ritual virgin worshiping, claiming it is a deprivation of childhood. They say that upon her inevitable retirement, the Nepalese girl who was once maximally coddled, will live in permanent post-goddess distress. I've always been skeptical of culture-neutral activism: campaigns touting universal definitions of human rights to achieve the incurious sterilization of an offending custom. In *World Policy Journal,* Shashi Tharoor reminds us that "in the Confucian or Vedic traditions, duties are considered more important than rights, while in Africa it is the community that protects and nurtures the individual." The imperatives of culture-neutral activism are characteristically incompatible with the social legacy of the Kumari tradition. The campaign is an indefensible replication of the degeneracy of colonialism: smudging one culture as it implicitly burnishes its own.

There are as many as eleven Kumaris throughout Nepal at a given time, but the Raj Kumari who dwells in Kumari Ghar is, perfunctorily, Nepal's most important person. Throughout the country—from the *terai* (plains) to the *pahad* (hills) to the *himal* (mountains)—there are innumerable temples with statues depicting the Hindu Pantheon. The granite edges of the statues are worn by the eager palms of their supplicants, so imagine the lure of a living deity.

Kumari's main duty is to embody. She is an incarnation of Taleju (aka Durga, the mother goddess (who is an incarnation of Devi (the feminine divine))). We squint at the window, the Hindu priest and I, and there are others too, still deciding on whether they'll stay or go. We are looking into the young girl's dwelling. She is kindergarten age. I transpose the priest to the suburbs of Pennsylvania, imagine him outside the window of my small cousin's bedroom. She'll be twelve this year. How quickly he would be ambushed by the North Huntingdon Police for suspicions of voyeurism. In Durbar Square, though, it is a

Nepalese police officer who enthusiastically leads me to the spot beneath the girl's window.

"I was here in February when the old Kumari. Now, it's new Kumari," the priest says. He seems like a decent man.

II.

A week ago, I night-hiked the Trikuta Mountains of India to the Vaishno Devi Temple. At the peak, thousands of fatigued pilgrims silenced their mantra ("mataji") and single-filed into a tunnel that ends in a cave inside which is the *sanctum sanctorum*. This is where, according to the Shri Mata Vaishno Devi Shrine Board, "the Divine Mother has revealed Herself in a natural rock form known as the Holy Pindies." Men and women alike had devoted hours of aerobic energy to worship these sacred stones, geological manifestations of the feminine divine.

As I stared at the *pindies*, I couldn't help but think they looked like small landscaping rocks. I had been primed to accept the moment as one of transcendental importance, but as the priests shoved the pilgrims ahead of me to ensure there was no lingering, trying to maintain a continuous pace, I deferred to the mechanics of protocol, forgetting to treasure the sight of the *pindies*. I had even been given a few seconds longer to view the stones, the priests expecting the steep learning curve of my cultural literacy.

My descent into Katra was mute. Why did *I* not fall desperately to my knees and crawl to the finish line (as the woman before me had)? Later, I discovered a black market photograph of the *pindies* on eBay for $395. E-commerce is a pilgrimage of instant gratification.

III.

When Kumari menstruates, is it the girl or the goddess who "becomes a woman"? Regardless, her tenure ends, and the pilgrims gather to see the new Kumari. We wait, but the windows stay still. I conjure scenes of upraised royalty.

[6/15/94] *Rex Leo:* …recall Rafiki's anointment of Simba, the presentation on Pride Rock ("Aaaaah zabenya!" Zulu for Royal royal).

[11/19/02] *Rex Stragulum:* …or the tabloid fodder of the King of Pop at Hotel Adlon, hoisting Blanket Jackson over the heads of gawping Berliners.

[3/31/14] *Rex Anglie:* …or the first official portrait of Prince George of Cambridge at eight months, future king perched in a window of Kensington Palace with mom Katherine, dad William, and royal spaniel, Lupo.

[12/25/14] *Rex Iudaeorum:* …or the telecast of Pope Francis from the central balcony of St. Peter's Basilica, declaring Jesus is born.

At 10:30 a.m., I start to feel indignant, entitled. Where's Kumari? I start to feel like the jilted Lloyd Dobler, standing in the boom box frame of *Say Anything*. The priest has distanced himself from me via some imperceptible moonwalk across the courtyard. Just barely out of comfortable conversational range, he chats with an acquaintance in Nepalese. I feel my cheeks loosen as they forfeit the smile.

Culled from the Sakhya caste, Kumari candidates must possess all thirty-two *lachchins* (Hindi for "characteristics"). What begins as pageantry (a Vedic *Toddlers and Tiaras*) develops into a harrowing scene. The prepubescent finalist, sometimes as young as two, attends the festival of Daishain. Thousands of animals are slain in the name of Kali, and fresh-severed heads of water buffaloes and goats are dragged into the blood-spattered courtyard of Taleju Temple, where the candidate is tested. Votives glint in the animal skulls as men chant and stagger, demon masks fixed to their faces. If the candidate shows any signs of fear, she is dismissed. If fearless, though, she is given the dubious privilege of bedroom quarantine with the severed heads.[1] I

---

[1] "[She] must wait… in order to claim her dubious privilege." (Gayatri Spivak, 'Can the Subaltern Speak?', 1988)

imagine her wide-eyed and forsaken in a strange room, the gloss of buffalo eyes the only thing reflecting in the darkness, maws half-opened so as to induce the unnerving tinnitus of Daishain din—scream and squawk and bleat. If she is tearless through dawn, her last test is to correctly identify Kumari's apparel from an assorted garment heap. At every stage, men ultimately decide the candidate's suitability for the position.

Activists insist Kumari is a job (i.e., child labor), but this presupposes an atheistic worldview. If she *is* a living goddess? Of the Nepalese I casually ask, most believe her incarnation is authentic. As far as they're concerned, her rites supersede her rights, meaning the domestic reality is that the Kumari regimen is god labor, not child labor.

Where is Kumari? Does she not want to take part in this fleet staring contest? Is mine an undue pressure? One thought anchors me to the courtyard for the duration: if when she looks out and the courtyard is empty, no one waiting for her, she may be crushed. I want to be a sample of the society into which she will eventually return.

Even before it turns 11 a.m., I know she won't be appearing today. The promise of the corporeal Durga disintegrates into *pindies*. The Hindu priest shrugs goodbye to me. I glance at the windows one last time: nothing.

IV.

On the taxi ride back to Thamel, the driver asks if I saw Kumari.

"I waited in Kumari Chowka, but she didn't appear. Not today."

"You can go tomorrow," he says, trying to negotiate a new fare. "I will pick you up at Annapurna Guesthouse in the morning."

"No. I leave tomorrow," I say with a quiver of relief, thumbing my iPod in the backseat.

"You should have paid her caregivers," the driver gives me too-late advice. "They would have let you see her in private."

Of course. It sounds pimpish at first, paying for Kumari's company, but it's just an extension of the hidden economy of South Asian tourism. I've paid enough of these discreet tolls by now to know that one can always circumvent the excesses of bureaucracy, be casually ushered into the streamline. It hadn't occurred to me, though, that I could pay admission to see a goddess. Tomorrow, when I exchange my unspent rupees, I'll wonder what pittance would have afforded her company.

I have seen photographs of Kumari in her palanquin, toes covered in rupees at festivals like Indra Jatra. Nepal's political leaders have paid her obeisance for centuries, from King Malla to the last modern king, Gyanendra. At any given moment, Kumari's horoscope must be aligned with the leader of Nepal; it legitimizes her annual anointment of the king. The girl presses the vermillion *tikala* onto his forehead, sustaining his right to rule. Since the Maoist uprising transformed Nepal's longstanding monarchy into a republic in 2008, Raj Kumari has been anointing Nepal's first and only president, Ram Baran Yadav.

What most ruffles *me* about Kumari is not the menace of child labor (see *god labor*), but the emptiness of her rigorous gestures. In *Discipline and Punish*, Michel Foucault suggests, "discipline produces subjected and practiced bodies, 'docile' bodies." If by being selected Kumari is transformed into a symbolic vessel, then it is an oblique sentencing. Kumari becomes the docile body politic—incarcerated, immobilized, uneducated. Her metatarsals, upon which the president lays his head, become ceremonial; due to the moratorium on locomotion, they are prone to fracture, a "political anatomy of detail" meant only to reconfirm presidential power. She becomes what cultural theorist, Gayatri Spivak, has called a pious item[2]

I shop for postcards in Thamel, rifle past Everest and stupa, prayer flags and temple, yak and macaque. There is a postcard

---

[2] "There is no virtue in global laundry lists with 'woman' as a pious item." (Gayatri Spivak, 'Can the Subaltern Speak?', 1988)

of the retired Kumari.[3] I buy it for my little cousin whose first menses is anon. I will tell her that "Kumari is ostensibly the most important person in the entire country of Nepal."

V.

As the constitution was drafted in 2008, Nepal's legislative parliament was comprised of a robust one-third representation by women. However, *The Kathmandu Post* reports that the preexisting patriarchal mode of Nepalese politics endured through the creation of the new republic. Savitra Bhusal said, "Whenever we [women] raise an issue… senior leaders walk out of the hall without caring to listen to us." Like Kumari, the parliamentary representation of feminine influence on daily life in Nepal is mostly symbolic. To see it any other way would require what Spivak calls "nativism or reverse ethnocentrism." These attitudes do not just exist in palaces and parliament, but they reverberate throughout all of Nepal—in the *terai*, the *pahad*, and the *himal*.

For instance, a Hindu woman in Nepal is customarily exiled to a rudimentary hut for several days each month (the duration of her menstruation), forced to live in austerity, eating a simple diet, not bathing, and sequestered from the company of her husband so that she does not contaminate her household. In this practice known as *chhaupadi* (outlawed in 2005, but still prevalent in rural Nepal), menstruation is cause for banishment. For young girls experiencing their period for the first time, *chhaupadi* lasts for one-third of a month. This tradition is echoed in Kumari's retirement; traditionally, upon being exiled from the palace, the girl returns to her home after years of being away but is not permitted into the courtyard. The residue of the latest goddess leaves her while she shivers in the *chhaupadi* shed.

---

[3] "Yesterday I was a living god of Nepal, but now I am a normal girl. I'm a little sad I'm not a god anymore." (Samita Bajracharya, *Maclean's*, 2014)

VI.

In her essay "Can the Subaltern Speak?" Gayatri Spivak writes about the duality of Sati and sati. While the former is the name of the goddess who self-immolated due to mortification (her father lambasted her husband), the latter is a funerary practice in which a widow self-immolates on her husband's funeral pyre. Spivak denounces the colonial campaign that interdicted *sati*, calling it imperialist, "[erasing] the image of the luminous fighting Mother Durga and [investing] the proper noun Sati with no significance other than the ritual burning of the helpless widow as sacrificial offering who can then be saved." *Sati*, which was uniformly banned throughout India by the mid-nineteenth century, was still permitted in Nepal until 1920.

Spivak renounces goddess pilgrimages as "proof of the feminism of classical Hindiusm"; to her, goddess-centered is not *ipso facto* feminist especially since the origin of most sacred pilgrimages to the feminine divine are inscribed by male gods' shattering of the female body. Too, reciting the *Mataji* mantra ("respected mother") is just lip service—not any more feminist than the male gaze during a mudwrestling match is a celebration of female athletics. No matter whose "protection" she is under, Spivak concludes "there is no space from which the sexed subaltern subject can speak."

The first time I read this line, her disciplined conclusion, I optimistically assumed Spivak was playing devil's advocate. I waited for some ethical parlor trick to unfold.

Later, I read it as a desperate call to arms, but activism primarily encourages actors to further act upon the subaltern and her culture. The impulse to "fix" is often a preservative for her voicelessness.

Now, when I read it, the essay is a stethoscope, an acoustic instrument pressed against the neck of the subaltern whose larynx has been systematically removed. Spivak's deconstruction explicitly states the subaltern and her voice are mutually exclusive: should she find it, she ceases to be subaltern.

VII.

In *Weapons of the Weak: Everyday Forms of Peasant Resistance*, James C. Scott documents the lesser-known arsenal of "ordinary weapons of relatively powerless groups":

> foot dragging, dissimulation, desertion, false compliance, pilfering, feigned ignorance, slander, arson, sabotage, and so on… They require little or no coordination or planning; they make use of implicit understandings and informal networks; they often represent a form of individual self-help; they typically avoid any direct, symbolic confrontation with authority.

In these everyday actions, one can find the dramatization of a "constant, grinding conflict" as opposed to the "rare heroic." I am reminded of how in 2007, Burmese monks refused alms from Myanmar's oppressive military junta, invoking a rite called *patam nikkuijana kamma* (or "turning over the rice bowl"). Because in the Pali tradition, giving [rice] is a way of receiving [karma], the monks' actions were perceived as a hostile repudiation of top Burmese generals. These subtle means of individual and collective resistance can initiate change within a culture as deemed necessary by that culture. Separately, Scott lists linguistic weapons of the weak: "rumour, gossip, disguises, linguistic tricks, metaphors, euphemisms, folktales, ritual gestures, and anonymity."

The weakest form and most effective form of resistance I can imagine for Kumari is amenorrhea ("absence of menstruation"). Consider the amenorrheic reign of an incumbent goddess, a kumari who stays Kumari.

VIII.

For the first time in over two-and-a-half centuries, due to a referendum, Raj Kumari is receiving an education. This is perhaps why she did not appear at the window while I waited—a lengthy lesson or an exam. As she gets older, I imagine her civic studies will incite curiosity:

Why do 'senior leaders walk out' when the women of Parliament speak?
Why are there so few female ministers and female committee members?
What is the root cause of the systemic violence against Nepalese women?

I imagine an amenorrheic Kumari whose palatial education pro-
tracts into politicization. She could weaponize the ritual gesture
of anointment, withhold the *tikala* until the president's ear has
leaned into her lips (and by extension, the lips of every Nepalese woman), until he has internalized their collective silence,
acknowledged their status as vote bank. She could force him
into public promise, make him work for his symbol of anointment, make him beg for his *tikala*. She could turn him into a
docile body until he admits that even Parliament's *chhaupadi* shed
is still in service.

The anomalous figure of an amenorrheic kumari may seem
hopelessly aspirational—its implausibility further muting the
subaltern—but she wouldn't be the first. After I return to the
States, I realize Patan currently has two Kumaris, one of whom
is sixty-three-year-old Dhan Kumari whom the *Kathmandu Post*
refers to as "eternally divine." Born in the *Kingdom* of Nepal,
Dhan Kumari's marathon incumbency precedes the ideal of kumari amenorrhea in the fledgling *Federal Democratic Republic* of
Nepal as she lacks the formal education being afforded the newest goddess.

IX.

If my first (and only) appearance at the *ghar* was unsure—a curiosity about one girl's captivity, a way to kill time—then only
now, a year later, am I stepping away. When I inevitably return
to Kathmandu, I won't revisit the *ghar*. I won't pay her keepers
their rupees nor will I will pay her obeisance. I won't be the one
to coax her into ceremonial pantomime because her position
has finally been potentiated by the culture that so resoundingly
cherishes it. The vacancy of the *chhaupadi* hut depends on Kumari's empty courtyard. I will not see her in flesh, but in text: the

litany of kumari *lachchins* (characteristics):

1. straight, right
2. but turns
3. round head
4. broad forehead
5. neck like a conch
6. lashes of a cow
7. black blue eyes
8. forty teeth
9. shapely teeth
10. white teeth
11. small tongue
12. moist tongue
13. the deep voice of a sparrow
14. cheeks of a lion
15. neck
16. strong body
17. resembling banyan trees
18. pure body
19. formed like a deer
20. chest of a lion
21. round shoulders
22. long arms
23. cont. supple hands
24. feet of a duck
25. cont. supple feet
26. feet under the sole
27. well-formed feet
28. supple feet
29. thighs of a deer
30. genitals positioned deep in the pelvis
31. beautiful shadow
32. copper-tinted nails
33. yellow shadow
34. feet of a
25. cont. tender feet
25. Saptaachata
5. beautiful skin tone
30. long toes

[4] Text from Niloufar Nouaven, "Enquete Sur Les Kumari," *Kailash*. 1974.
Adapted from "Les 2 Signes Ou Battislaksana."

Azimuth as a Myth:
A Lyric Algorithm For
an Off-Brand GPS

I.

Today, a solar flare is scheduled to cause disruptions in electromagnetic fields. The filament in the sun's Corona will affect transmissions to receivers. Some models of GPS may present drivers with counterintuitive directions. Drivers are advised to cross-reference travel itineraries with analog maps. Beware: certain adapters not recommended for use with this product. Those made in Cambodia and Vietnam for instance. If the unit short circuits, it will trigger a deleterious algorithm.

II.

If my GPS ever glitches (best-case scenario): I hope it takes me through a guardrail gap to the high desert plains. I want to go where professional drivers drift and weave sports cars and luxury sedans through soft sand coulees, narrowly missing strategically positioned cameramen. Imagine my meek commercial bomb due to GPS malfunction, a CR-V only one pixel tall floating left to right in Arizonan Tunisia. I'll be primetime's best-kept secret in the background of Audi's depiction of nowhere. If my GPS ever glitches (worst-case scenario): if it dictates a hairpin turn that isn't there and my tires scream off a sheer cliff, I will blame (in this order): the voice actor whose phonemes have been strung into geosemantic units; the programmer whose negligence is as good as manslaughter; the sun and its solar flare; a technophilic culture that conspired to encourage my father—a man who is neither predisposed to give nor receive gifts—to purchase and gift me the off-brand GPS that acted more as weapon than navigation system. He shook my hand and said,

"Make sure you program it *before* you hit the road."

III.

NOTHING, AZ (road to nowhere) / I am trying to resolve the paradox of "the road to nowhere." On Arizona Highway 93, there is a place called Nothing. The village, once inhabited by four people, is now completely abandoned. Next to the sole garage, there's a sign that reads "Nowhere, Arizona." The sign sits on terra, faithfully adheres to the coordinate plane: 34°28'47"N' 113°20'7"W'. The road to Nothing approaches nowhere like an asymptote, continuously destining.

IV.

In Pixar's *Cars*, the anthropomorphized racecar protagonist Lightning McQueen tells his agent, "I'm in this little town called Radiator Springs. You know Route 66? It's still here!" It's a giddy moment. The relic route is resurrected. I paused the movie and stood up for the first time all day just to look at the parked cars at Tucson High's stadium lot. Lightning's agent dismisses the detour as play, though. "Yeah, that's great, kid. Playtime is over, pal."

V.

KINGMAN, AZ (wrong turn) / It is getting harder and harder to get lost. North of Nothing, after breakfast in Kingman, Cory and I—on our way to Vegas—miss the entrance ramp for the highway. We end up in an alley. There are chipped statues of Jesus and the Virgin of Guadalupe. There are fenced pit bulls pacing their lots. A half-dozen lawn mowers are queued under a carport. We wonder why so many lawnmowers since all the yards are all dirt. "Wow. Those mowers really did their job," Cory says. At the end of the alley, we make a dead-end turn and face a piece of graffitied plywood that reads: You miss you. One of us starts to cry. Later in memory, we say we didn't stop at the plywood, but burst through it.

VI.

If you really scrutinize a map, you may be lucky enough to find a phantom settlement, a copyright trap inserted by cartographers to catch would-be plagiarists. The cartographer knows what it takes to be unlocatable. To be a phantom. To be a timorous population of one. I hope the last person on Earth was a solipsist all along.

VII.

LAS VEGAS, NV / Fuck Las Vegas.

VIII.

When I received a $350 fine for driving alone in the HOV lane in Phoenix, I half-joked with the officer, asked if she would consider considering the GPS a sort of passenger. She nearly gave me a field sobriety test. It is a peculiar disappointment to have someone take your half-joke as full-joke. GPS *is* the invisible woman. GPS is She-PS is fantasy lover, fetishized machine, keeping company on remote stretches. GPS is Marco, and I am pulling over to imagine the actual distance between us, not as a cupric cartoon vein on a map, but an untraveled pastoral inverse. Sometimes, it feels as if I'm stalking her, chasing her to the destination, where she is waiting with champagne or ice water. She teases with coquettish directives. I imagine her battery life (73%) in parallel flux as I caffeinate then fatigue, caffeinate then fatigue. I imagine she looks like a solar flare, an orb of intense brightness exceeding the visible light spectrum. I imagine she looks like my ex-fiancée who's left me for Tonopah, Nevada—a superscript of white joules extended from the solar limb, sequestered in silo. Out of sight, detonated in mind.

Plagiarism templates courtesy of Thompson, Kerouac, and Steinbeck: We were somewhere around [place name], on the edge of the desert, when the drugs began to take hold… With the coming of [person name] began the part of my life you could call my life on the road… When I was very young and the urge to be someplace else was on me, I was assured by mature people that [abstract concept] would cure this itch…

Kingman	Cory	self-actualization
Nothing	Cory	marriage
Las Vegas	Cory	apocalypse
Seligman	Cory	Dào
Tonopah	Cory	Gold Bond Rapid Relief Anti-Itch Cream

X.

SELIGMAN, AZ (birthplace of a road) / "IMG_1077.jpg" has endured several rounds of deletion due to its enigmatic right corner blur. I set the self-timer, propped the camera on the side-view mirror, and sprinted toward the sign, announcing Seligman (population: 456) as "Birthplace of Route 66." There is a blur following me like the tail of a comet. I leaned on the left side of the sign. My ex-fiancée leaned on its right. As if both of us were holding it up. The six feet of aluminum sign felt like the halfway point to the 619 miles that would soon divide us. Months after the photo was taken, Route 66 became road-cum-severer, road-cum-culprit, road-cum-perpetrator of long distances, eternal dotted span with manifold mirages of ferret, horse, and hare. I've known a road to be a kind of weapon. I've used the road as an excuse (look, its cruel magnitude). I've held the road up as an emblem of withdrawal. Before we left Seligman, we listened to a family with three squealing kids encircling salvaged cars. The boy's father quoted Lightning McQueen from Cars in his best Owen Wilson-as-Lightning impression: "You've got more talent in one lug nut that a lot of cars has got on their whole body." The eldest son asked what a lug nut was, and the father tried to explain. The film's fictional town, Radiator Springs, was based on the main drag of Seligman. My ex-fiancée and I eavesdropped as children asked naïve questions about the remoteness of Seligman, about the disuse of Route 66. Based on their answers, it was unclear if the parents found Seligman romantic or revolting.

XI.

NEVADA NATIONAL SECURITY SITE, NV (*classified roads*) / In Nye County, Nevada (home to the largest zero-population land tract of the 2000 United States census, home to Tonopah too), the cell phone dead zones stretch for miles. Here, it really is just me with GPS. She disappears at times, goes searching for signal while I count Joshua trees. There are margins made of stainless steel, guardrails keeping me from stray. I heed the dotted line. The narcoleptic truckers percuss the rumble strip like a rubber-buffeted alarm. Delta sleep deficiencies. Technology will return as sweetheart, beguile with humanoid phonemes, count down miles and minutes. Car acoustics. I eat the fig paste cookies (hot from console oven) and four sticks of cinnamon chewing gum. While on tour of the Nevada National Security Site, the van visits the crater pocks left behind by kiloton blasts still coated with residual radiation. We're shown photos of the mushroom-tipped clouds and war-era propaganda in support of nuclear proliferation. We drive the perimeter of a containment area of low-grade nuclear waste. The network of discreetly labeled roads is a careful history lesson, but my eyes are drawn to the periphery of the tour, to the carefully avoided roads that we bypass, TS/SCI roads requiring DOD credentials, roads leading to inaccessible sites with well-guarded military, nuclear, and UFO secrets, roads whose destinations are civilian nowheres. Not even Google Earth permits.

XII.

Map says, *You are here*. But even when I'm not, even when I'm elsewhere, the map's text is static, insisting. Sometimes, when no one is looking at the map, the map speaks to no one, says to no one, *You are here*, even when no one is intrinsically nowhere. I crave a map that can show me—precisely and efficiently— where I am not, to infect me with longing, wanderlust. When looking into the rear-view mirror—the picture window and its delicate inventory—geography and time are compressed. Passed becomes past becomes

Too Slow Is How That Tortoise Go:
A Carapace in 37 Parts

[1] If when you slept on your chest, your spine became a roof: a tortoise. I count the carapace's scutes as my finger runs across each ridge like a roadway. The slow scrape of fingernail on tortoiseshell, the keratin-on-keratin caress, is like tires made of asphalt, or a road of rubber. How lightly I would travel on a highway that could sense me upon it.

[2] "Scute" comes from the Latin plural *scuta*, meaning shields. There are three types of scutes: marginal, costal, and vertebral. They are like shingles covered in nerve endings and pores. I imagine the nuchal bone above his neck as cornerstone. (Note: A mason uses three types of stone to construct snecked rubble: risers, levelers, and snecks. Snecks are smaller stones used to fill in the gaps created by the uneven placement of the larger stones.)

[3] In *The Golden Bough*, James Frazer writes that a modern Greek builder sometimes "entices a man to the [cornerstone], secretly measures his body… or his shadow, and buries the measure under the foundation-stone; or he lays the foundation-stone upon the man's shadow." Within a year, the man is expected die.

[4] While in Cambodia for thirty days—the longest I had ever left my tortoise in someone else's care, the floor of the guesthouse utterly without his roving shell, the heat-seeking swivel of the familiar turtleneck—I cultivated an obsession to reduce my anxiety. Walking past the fish vendors of Psar Chaa, I inhaled the brine as I watched the prawn swimmerets wriggle in mid-air. Black eels corkscrewed into one other, forming intricate

helixes. Carp flopped from chopping block to concrete. At one intersection, I stopped at a red bucket of turtles. One climbed on the back of his docile peers and did a brave chin-up to the plastic rim. With a long knife, the vendor flipped the turtle onto its back.

[5] From my knees, I zoom, focus and shoot each scute. The nuchal bone is the most difficult to photograph as it is only entirely visible when he retreats inside himself. Inches away, I must kneel, lean and torque for a full glimpse. The shadow of my forearm darkens the frame, prolongs the exposure and inevitably blurs the shot. Just as any place I've ever lived—those structures—will likely outlast me, so too will my Greek tortoise. I try not to see it this way.

[6] The first tortoise I ever saw belonged to my neighbor, Yuichi. His tortoise, Koopa, was always shinier than mine. Named after the turtle soldiers of the *Mario* series, Koopa was regularly polished with Turtle Wax Express Shine car detailer Yuichi found in the garage. When Yuichi moved away, I wrote to him. *How's Koopa?* I asked. (Call your local poison control center.)

[7] It may be for certain that "carapace" comes from the Greek *appa* ("cape"). In her book of essays *The Deep Zoo*, Rikki Ducornet explains, "a creature with a shell is a mixed creature; it reveals and conceals itself simultaneously."

[8] I was five the first time I counted to one hundred; I immediately started over and did it again—sometimes just to fall asleep in these finite carnations until I lost consciousness. After one hundred, I regressed to counting on my fingers for 101, 102, etc. The unsurety of another digit. I pinched down on the keratin of my index nail, middle nail, etc.

[9] In his article, "Scutes and Age Determination of Desert Tortoises Revisited," David Germano notes that for tortoises up

to seven years old, each scute has "the exact number of [rings] as age." By age twenty, though, the number of rings is one less than the tortoise's ago. Caveat: As if protein can only count so high no scute has more than twenty-five rings.

[10] In a grove in Muir Woods, the rings of a twelve-hundred-year-old redwood, its bark circumtread by banana slugs (see dendrochronology v. scutachronology).

[11] In 1918, Victor David Brenner sculpted *A Song to Nature*, a fountain depicting the Greek god Pan reclining as he listens to a nymph playing the lyre. Beneath them, water flows from the beaks of four turtles perched over a granite font. I passed this fountain hundreds of time at the University of Pittsburgh, from all angles, on the way to or from the apartment room where I offered my Greek tortoise 10'x12' of carte blanche. (Don't tell the landlord.) While Brenner's bronze nymph was anonymous by design, I had at some decided for him that she was Chelone, asserting as much on official campus tours.

[12] Here, I further corrupt Chelone's myth: "Here, at the fountain, you can watch as Chelone plays the lyre for Pan. Chelone, who has just been invited to Zeus's wedding (see *The Aeneid*, is delaying, dilly-dallying, the only wedding guest not preparing for Zeus's big day. Look at her feet, where the spitting turtles foreshadow her punishment just as she (her name) foreshadows their taxonomy (turtles, of the order Cheloni). The water screams have their own shadows. In Aesop's Fables, the tortoise RSVPs, 'Be it ever so humble, there's no place like home.' If you stand long enough at this fountain, wait for Chelone's 'song to nature' to conclude, you will witness Zeus clapping Chelone's house onto her back. Condemned to stay at home forever, it is the ultimate uninvitation." I've made peace with my mythic invention, deciding Brenner—who will forever be known as the designer of the Lincoln cent anyway, that gleaming presidential profile in zinc + copper bas-relief—would likely not

have minded.

[13] More anciently, according to Hindu Mythology, for one millennium the gods and demons—craving the nectar of immortality, Amrita—churned the Ocean of Milk. In depictions of the churning, it appears as if the gods and demons are in an epic tug-of-war context. The churning string, the serpent-king Vasuki, is wound around Mount Mandara. The gods pull the serpent's tail and the demons pull its head, and the mountain begins to spin, thus churning the ocean. Before the nectar flows, though, the mountain sinks into the ocean. Vishnu appears as Kurma, the tortoise avatar (#2 of 10 in the Dashavatara sequence). According to Canto Eight of *Bhagavata Purana*, Vishnu "expanded Himself into the wondrous body of a giant tortoise," and swimming into the water, he took the mountain onto his back so that Mount Mandara looked "like a continent." The gods and demons recommenced their churning, and the tortoise "considered it an infinitely pleasant scratching."

[14] In the 1990s, due to the success of the Teenage Mutant Ninja Turtles franchise, Britain saw a 750% increase in its red-eared slider population. In an article in *The Daily Beast*, conservationist Pauline Kidner describes how, after the initial enthusiasm for the new pet dulled, parents would often release the turtles into waterways, sewer-bound (you know, to where their rat sensei live?), and the turtles wrecked havoc on "the ecosystem, eating ducklings, small water birds and other amphibians."

[15] Unlike aquatic turtles, most tortoises are herbivorous. The desert tortoise requires a diet high in keratin. When I go too long without clipping my toenails, they begin to resemble—in the right light—white hibiscus petals, and my tortoise nibbles at them.

[16] The first time I saw a wild tortoise in the Sonoran Desert, I thought I had encountered a zombie. Its beak was covered, I

thought, in red blood. Was it an omnivore after all? What small mammal had it managed to apprehend at just two-tenths of a mile per hour? Something grievously wounded. I later saw the trail of prickly pear cacti their mutilated wine-red fruit faucets of jam.

[17] When my girlfriend asks me what color she should paint her toenails, I shrug and tell her, unhelpfully, "Not yellow" (color of bell peppers, dandelions, and squash).

[18] What mortar coheres this carapace? He sleeps in a corner in the shadow of many limbs—desk legs, chair legs, my legs—huddled next to a hunk of petrified wood that I once used as a paperweight.

[19] In *Paper Mario*, Koopa Troopa proclaims, "This shell was made to order. That's why it fits me so well. I mean, how cool do I look?" The turtle soldiers retreat inside their green shells when Mario jumps on them. Virtually indestructible, the shells can only be destroyed by fireball or rainbow.

[20] During Pol Pot's agrarian socialist crusade in Cambodia, the Khmer Rouge set millions of landmines. It is estimated that four to six million still remain. Imagine the slow-moving yellow-headed tortoise on Cambodian plains, moving unconsciously toward or away from its own detonation. A few kilograms are all it takes to detonate a landmine. An adult yellow-headed tortoise can weight up to 3.5 kilograms—almost or just barely enough, depending. The Khmer conservationist has become as endangered as the species she aims to conserve.

[21] A tortoise without its shell would look like a miniature dinosaur—a Brontosaurus, I think.

[22] As the landmines burst from below, the United States carpet-bombed Cambodia from above. President Nixon's chief of

staff, H.R. Haldeman, wrote in his diary "K really excited, as is P." That's Kissinger and President. A double amputee grunted at me while I was walking through Wat Botum Park in Phnom Penh. Between his teeth, he held a decades-old photograph of himself with arms. I put a U.S. dollar in the chest pocket of his vest, and he caressed me with his stump. With one of the highest rates of amputation in the world, it is hard to share K and P's zeal of their secret operation in Cambodia.

[23] The longest-living Greek tortoise was named Timothy. She was born the year Louis Daguerre's daguerreotype "Boulevard du Temple" was taken (1893); it is the oldest known photograph with human subjects. Timothy died at the age of one hundred sixty-fixe the same year Facebook was launched (2004); with over six billion monthly uploads, it is the largest photo-sharing site in the world.

[24] Few people know that Timothy the Tortoise was actually female, born before naturalists knew how to sex a tortoise. She is buried in Devon, England, the following words etched to her underside plastron: "Where have I fallen? What have I done?"

[25] In a classic NOFX song, "Timothy the Turtle," Fat Mike relinquishes lead vocals to Duncan, the British singer from Snuff. "Timmy the Turtle" is pronounced "Tam-maythe Tur-hul." This is how I imagine Timothy's closest friends in Devon greeted her.

[26] "The Boulevard du Temple" daguerreotype captures Paris's 3rd arrondissement at midday. Whereas a relatively long ten-second exposure would at least leave evidence of the thoroughfare's cabriolet carriage and pedestrian traffic by way of vector streaks, this photograph's patient ten-minute exposure depicts only a population of two: a man having his boots polished by another man on the sidewalk's corner. They are surrounded by road beneath them, trees around them, and buildings above them while all else is bleached by velocity.

[27] Even though he moves so slowly, at least half of the six hundred photographs of my tortoise have a detectable motion blur, an illusion of briskness, an abortive irony.

[28] "Too sloooow/ is how the that turtle go." Fat Mike chimes in, snotty as ever, reclaiming the pronunciation in the chorus. I the *45 of 46 Songs that Weren't Good Enough to Go on Our Other Records* liner notes, Fat Mike writes of *Timmy the Turtle* EP, "We didn't press that many cuz [sic] the songs [sic] not very good and we didn't think we'd sell very man."

[29] A Greek riddle: "While alive I was silent, dead I sing sweetly." (Hint: The first harps were made of tortoise shells.)

[30] I used to think people died when they turned a hundred. Turns out—being average, being American, being male—I'll die at seventy-eight.

[31] My dad wants to be cremated; he thinks embalming is too similar to taxidermy.

[32] Depending on which country I am in, I will sometimes believe in reincarnation (though never in America, which is so seduced by death; its drip of life insurance commercials, "if it bleeds, it leads" headlines, the fetish of the American hostage, Mom calling to tell me my friend's mom is dead).

[33] Methuselah, who was the grandfather of Noah, died at the age of 969. I imagine Methuselah reincarnated as a mayfly. A mayfly, of the order *ephemeroptera* (literally "day-long" + "wing"), typically dies within twenty-four hours of hatching. Actually: the irony would still be intact if Methuselah were reincarnated as anything at all because just seven days after his death, the skies opened for the Great Flood.

[34] Because my father has already purchased a plot in the cem-

etery, I know someday I will to confront him about the discrepancy, demand clarity regarding how his remains should remain.

[35] At the temple complex of Angkor Wat, I walk among French, English, Dutch, Chinese, Indian, Korean, and Khmer pilgrims along the corridors of the galleried architecture, looking for the limestone bas-relief frieze of Samudra Manthan, of the Churning of the Ocean of Milk. Turning corners at the end of long corridors, I repeatedly encounter the same Khmer man. It feels like we're both looking for the same thing. By the third encounter, I almost wave. The Khmer man is an amputee, missing all of one arm and most of another.

[36] When I find the Samudra Manthan, I hoist the camera above my head and take many photographs. The Khmer man, curious to see what I am photographing, casually stands behind me. I am more aware of his frame than my own as he looks through my hoisting arms (limbs 1 & 2) to their shadows projected on the limestone (3 & 4), the chimera of Vishnu-as-Kurma in bas-relief with four arms (5-8) and two legs (9 & 10), the many muscled right arms of the gods (11-16 in frame) and muscled left arms of the demons (17-22 in frame) as they pull the churning rope, Vasuki. Or maybe the Khmer man just stares at the potent serpent-king, the limbless Vasuki. After being tugged at for millennia, Vasuki is moments away from vomiting tarlike venom into the ocean, poisoning the universe and spoiling the immortal nectar. When I turn to glance at the Khmer man, he is already gone; likely a Theravada Buddhist, he seems more inclined to stand before another of Vishnu's avatars, Buddha (#9 of 10 in the Dashavatara sequence). The temple complex is riddled with beheaded stone statues of Buddha; in a genocide that fetishized the uneducated proletariat, the Enlightened One became Public Enemy Number One.

[37] "Yes, you can pet him." I often hear myself giving friends permission. "On the carapace, on the head, on any which limb,

though this one—this front left—he'll likely draw in. That's where I sometimes plunge the syringe through the plates for his medicine. I mean, if you think he trusts you, and if you're starting to trust him too, then go ahead and pet him under the chin. That's his favorite spot, his number one excuse to come out of his shell."

Captioning Novitiate

Figs. 1 & 2. There will be a head-shaving today. Two boys;
one must go first. The novitiates must be of a certain age. Some
call it thirteen. Some call it ten. Some call it, "Can the child scare
a crow?" The boys demur as the adults stand by, making small
talk as they await the gridlock to resolve itself. Saying softly: *You
go first / No, you*—clinging to their hair for a few moments more.

Today has been declared an auspicious day to enter the monastery; a day to follow the path of Buddha's son, Rahula. Two
thousand and five hundred years ago, Rahula asked his father
for his inheritance. Instead, Buddha sheared his son's hair and
beckoned him into the forest monastery, and Rahula followed
without hesitation. Thus began the path of *sramanera*.

The elder monk, who, with whetstone and strop on a *hlu-win*,
honed the razor and examined its parts—handle, shoulder, back,
head, point, edge, blade, heel, shank, pivot, tang—is yawning
now in the shade of a tree, patiently rotating the razor, still waiting for the boys to decide who will be first.

The boys are polite to one another as they speak, true partners in this ceremonial tonsure, but each still clings to his hair. Eventually, one agrees to go first. He grinds his teeth as his head is soaked with water from a hose. On his haunches, frowning, his scalp is shorn in front of everyone. Tufts of black hair hallow the sand. Two friends becoming *sramanera*, following Rahula. Afterwards, they race in the yard, filling it with joyful cackling. Happy *shinbyu*, happy *shinbyu*.

Fig 3. In George Orwell's *Burmese Days*, the unscrupulous Burmese officer U Po Kyin intends to rectify his iniquity by spending his capital on a bevy of pagodas. Even after British colonialism in Burma ended in 1948, U Po Kyin's native greed resonated as the corrupt junta reigned through 2010. Though he dies before the first pagoda ever breaks the tree line, one can see—a hundred steps above the green Bago forest, conflagrated by semal trees' burst orange-buds—that many others have taken up U Po Kyin's mantle. Both a memorial and a reliquary, the pagoda is a ubiquitous architecture in Myanmar, which is also known as the "Land of Pagodas." I sense a pilgrimage that extends along Myanmar's national borders.

Looking out on the vastness, the gilded spires piercing the canopy, I imagine for a moment that I am alone. On the other side of the gold-flaked and sun-scorched central tower of this pagoda, however, I hear a group of young monks also making a pilgrimage. The child monks drink in the apparent boundlessness of "public." "Please take mine," one monk pleads, pointing to my camera.

In their first days away from home they are giddy at the prospect of further dislocation forged by their pagoda ascent. They warble with independence. Having circled the narrow belt around the tower, they look out at a giant Buddha reclined in right lateral-recumbent position. His shoulder bulges above the trees.

After the *shinbyu* ceremony in Bagan, a single mother invited me back to her home. Her daughter prepared snacks while her son presented me with a photograph of Barack Obama kissing the Burmese Nobel Prize laureate Aung San Suu Yki on the cheek. The mother was occupied rifling through identical DVD cases: she had an archive of all the local *shinbyu* ceremonies—presumably those of her nephews and nieces, the children of neighbors and friends, captured and duplicated via DVD burner. I ate their snacks while watching yet another *shinbyu*, another delicate tonsure: hose, razor, and the inevitable scalp. She pointed at her chest over and over again. "My," she said. I felt her son's absence sharply.

I see him through the viewfinder first. It's not her son, but somebody else's: head shorn, feet bare, saffron robe torqued, revealing navel, tongue out in a display of juvenilia, punctuating my panorama.

As he descends the stairs, I think of how his tongue—in this photograph at least—will never retract. The urban legend plays out: so a face can get stuck that way. Later, the driver tells me that in the monastery, a child monk will spend many hours in silence as if alone. *As if.*

Figs. 4, et al. After the milk rice was eaten, Buddha pitched the golden bowl into the river. The bowl floated upstream as if caught in a supernatural current or on the back of a river shark. In Myanmar, the Irrawaddy river flows south. It is essential for irrigation and trade. Not even the monsoon can reverse its course. Paddies flood. Rice grows, husks are milled, and grains polished. In a country whose public looks to the monastic community—the *sangha*—for spiritual and political leadership, perhaps only the sage can redirect the Irrawaddy's course, inspire the current to revolt.

At 7 a.m., following their teacher, the child monks, arranged by height, sloping like an asymptote to the earth's coordinate plane, hold bowls against their abdomens. The teacher strikes the bell, announcing the alms round, and laypeople convene in the town. To give alms is to gain merit. When enough moral capital is accumulated, in this incarnation or the next, one may attain nirvana. Nirvana comes from the Sanskrit *va*– ("to blow") and *nir*– ("out"); one never knows which grain will breach the threshold, invoke the wind that slips one through the microscopic pores of the "universal."

So the almsgivers are more grateful to give than the monks are to receive. It is one of the more perfunctory roles of the monk. In the instant of her giving, the almsgiver attains peak piety. Like U Po Kyin's promissory pagodas, one needs only to lift the veil of such spiritual practice to reveal the karmic economy. Despite being the poorest country in Southeast Asia, local Burmese are eager to purchase small flakes of gold, usually only one square centimeter at a time, to contribute to the girth of the golden *stupas*. According to the *Myanmar Times*, the Burmese have been buying gold leaf since the 1400s, which is when the Mon Queen, Shin Sawbu, "gave her weight in gold to Shwedagon," Myanmar's most expensive and holy (these superlatives are seemingly interchangeable) pagoda.

Minutes later, a monsoon gale transforms the concrete into a treadmill belt, and the pedestrians are caught in a static trek. The monks earn inches toward the monastery, their rice bowls covered.

On rare occasions, a monk will refuse alms. Such an act is a moral judgment of the would-be almsgiver. When it happens on a large scale, it can start a revolution. In 2007, after the junta overburdened Burmese citizens with an extortionate manipulation of the military's fuel monopoly, monks responded with the Saffron Revolution. Alms were summarily refused by some first monk who turned over his alms bowl (a monastic rite known as *patam nikkuijana kamma* in Pali, the sacred language of Theravada Buddhism), and the others followed, turning over their bowls too. As if to gently push the junta outside of the circle of the Buddhist faith, the monks instated a uniform bowl blockade to cease the flow of merit. Imagine the junta generals' faces flashing red in front of the monks' saffron robes.

Less than five years after the Saffron Revolution, Myanmar held long-awaited democratic by-elections, and the once illegal

National League for Democracy won 98 percent of the parliamentary seats. The *sangha*'s spiritual dissolution of the junta simultaneously led to its political dissolution. The Revolution, monsoon-like, effectively displaced the junta and extinguished the flames of self-immolation. In a reformed Myanmar, the *sangha* resumes its ancient spiritual regimen, and the path of *sramanera* is again unforked.

Sons of Sound:
A Lyric Concatenation for an Off-Brand GPS

Three women's voices are often telling me where to go. For almost a decade, I have been an occasionally lost dot way west of them. First, they must locate me. Each circle expands—Susan's (Atlanta), Karen's (New York City), and Mom's (Pittsburgh)—until I'm on its circumference. In a two-dimensional trilateration, I am the only point at which all three intersect. They speak in succession.

"You are 2,085 miles away from me," Satellite Susan says.

"You are 2,505 miles away from me," Satellite Karen says.

"You are 2,198 miles away from me," Satellite Mom says. "How could you?"

After he retired, Dad and I spent an hour each night lying across the bed, watching sports news television. Mom would call from her Ericson cell phone on the parkway, and Dad muted the television. Sportscaster Bob Pompeani's voice was replaced by Mom's muffled traffic updates. I assumed she was near Three

Rivers Stadium since, in my eight-year-old mind, the sports are-nas were coextensive with the Pittsburgh city limits. Jason Kendall crouched at home plate as consecutive silent slow-motion replays featured him tagging out an Orioles runner.

"Start eating dinner without me, if you want," Mom per-mitted. Even though I asked to speak to Mom, Dad would usu-ally hang up. Before unmuting the television, though, he often sang a song he had invented:

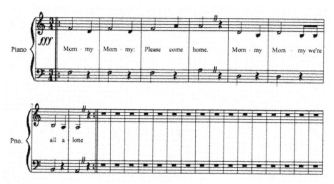

The pronoun is paradoxical: *we*'re all alone? I never understood how two people could be "all alone." Hadn't Harry Nilsson pro-claimed that one was the loneliest number? I retroactively revise the semantics so that "we're" means "he's," and the loneliness is projected solely upon me.

Almost twenty years later, and I'm living in California, lying across my bed, calling home. Dad, lying across his bed too, picks up. I ask what he's doing (watching sports news television). He asks if I saw the Steelers game (I hadn't). I ask if Mom is home (she isn't).

"So, you're all alone?" I ask him. It's supposed to be jocular, but his silence is existential.

"I am," he says eventually.

When I hang up, I resolve the paradox: if he sings from his bed and me from mine, each to Mom (who is gone, at her sister's), in ironic split-screen harmony, then *we* can be all alone.

Primary GPS: As a personal assistant, Susan's American English is accentless. She is generally supportive, though easily peeved, an eager referee of social etiquette. Her concatenation is relatively continuous, especially the diphthongs (e.g., Mountain, Trail, and Route), though pronunciation of words requiring uvular trills, alveolar trills, voiceless uvular fricatives, zeds, and the silent *h* are flawed and indifferent. In particular, non-Germanic words like entendre and aficionado are programmatically unthinkable. (see iPhone 5s)

Secondary GPS: Karen, on the other hand, lumbers through all pronunciations with an Australian English accent. Karen commands that I "torn roit onto Alhombra droiv," and does so with a high-rising terminal that registers as a lack of confidence, a question rather than a command. The concatenation is more jagged than Susan's, and random glottal stops, intoned as a metallic gurgle, bind most polysyllabic words. (see Garmin nüvi)

Second back-up GPS: Mom, a recently retired corporate secretary, picks up the phone, sounds out-of-breath as if just jogging the length of the house to receive me. She begins every conversation with a dutiful, "What's up?" as in "What can I help you with?" forfeiting her social utility. When Susan or Karen are unavailable, I call Mom, listen to her heavy breath as she descends stairs, treads hallways, and hovers over her keyboard. Susan and Karen have a fleet of NAVSTAR satellites trilaterating to locate me, but Mom's humble process is a cross-country hide-and-seek using MapQuest, zooming in and out until she's found my current intersection.

"Okay, I've got you," she says. "Now, where are you trying to get to?"

Mom's voice is natural, her pitch and speed purely her own, though her syllables are strung together with intervening bursts of breath, concatenated by dyspnea (shortness of breath), often chewing lozenges or gum as she speaks. Sometimes, I involuntarily round up her age and realize she's seventy.

She enters the address into the search field and reads the directive to me in a quavering voice. Her Appalachian accent is minimal (she is careful to avoid the general extender "n'at" and second person plural "yinz,"), though she does, on occasion, let slide some Pittsburghese, including the punctual "whenever" (as in "Whenever you reach the intersection…") and what Wisnosky (2003) has identified as the [c~a] merger (as in "Take the dahntahn exit"). Whereas Susan and Karen are silent as they wait for me to traverse the 1.6 miles between their directives, Mom goes off-script. She is kneeling on the couch, "neb-nosing" out loud, interposing the scene across the street from my childhood home with my current lostness in California.

"There are window cleaners," she says, and I ask, "Where?" as I drive through Sacramento, looking left and right.

"At the Jasko's," she clarifies.

Because of her nebbing, a brand new city can feel vaguely nostalgic. Some days, she tells me that across the street, my childhood friend Jaybo is home visiting his parents, his car parked perpendicular with our driveway, taunting her.

"Jay's home again this weekend," she says. "Why aren't you?" she doesn't say.

Sometimes, it feels as if she is directing me home, that if I acquiesce for a mere forty hours, she will direct me the entire 2,500 highway miles until my car is parked across the street from Jaybo's, two CR-Vs in parallel symmetry.

If voice is the vibration of white folds in the larynx, an organ made up of cartilage and muscle, stowed behind the flesh of the neck, incarcerated in epithelial cells, can it ever really be disembodied? A word like *dyspnea*—how to say it without the tongue, the palate, the teeth, and lips? Try *flanger* without the body. Try *friction*. Try *vivacity*, its anatomical ricochet.

On the way to the hardware store, driving through Midtown Sacramento, past its strands of valley oak and California sycamore, magnolia and elm, under ninety feet of continuous canopy, my GPS signal is obstructed. I have been relying on Mom more than ever to pick up Susan and Karen's slack. Their satellite searches can't penetrate the canopy, and Mom is eager to fill in as understudy, though sometimes I feel that my petty requests have nulled her retirement.

"Looks like you're going to have to turn around. Make your way toward Nineteenth Street," Mom says.

I maneuver westward and blame my dilemma on trivia. "Hey Mom, did you know Sacramento has more trees per capita than any other city in the World besides Paris?"

"I didn't," Mom says.

As I drive, Mom narrates the bird buffet in the backyard, all the feeders strung from willow boughs.

"Okay, I'm on Nineteenth," I say.

Just then, Susan speaks to me, quietly so Mom can't hear. She is directing me toward Ace Hardware too, and I'm conflicted: am I wasting Mom's time or making her feel useful?

"Wait, I lost you on the map," Mom says. She is zooming in and out, trying to relocate me. I tell her I'll pull over and wait, but keep driving. By the time she's found me again, I'm three-quarter miles closer to Ace. Even after I've parked in the lot, Mom is still dictating turns.

"You said left on I Street?" I ask Mom, watching several customers come and go through the doors, toting merchandise—a bamboo rake, compost bin, gas logs, and a combination leaf blower/vacuum/mulcher.

"Yeah," she says, oblivious. "In point-four miles."

"Okay. One sec," I say.

I endure the irony, mistaking it for covert generosity. Eventually, when I "arrive" again, I thank Mom, turn off the engine, and tell her I'll call her later.

When I was eight years old, my father snatched the glossy map out of my mother's hands. We were lost on vacation in D.C., curb-parked by the Department of Treasury. Moments earlier, I laughed as Dad, with some reluctance, spent his real money on a souvenir bag of shredded money. I squished it in the backseat as they argued. Dad gave me the map, a rhetorical demotion of Mom as navigator.

The District is a system, a grid of rectangles intersected by fifty-one avenues named for each state and Puerto Rico. My eyes gravitated toward the parks, plazas, and Potomac.

"How do we get out of here?" Dad tested me, and to this day, he swears I navigated us all the way home, though I remember it differently: a Middle Eastern gas station attendant pointing a finger while another man cleaned our windows with Windex and paper towels. When Dad told him to stop, that he didn't have any money, I didn't understand it was a bluff and felt guilty, hiding my souvenir beneath my legs. Dad rolled the window up, and with the tip of his index finger, FM radio began to crescendo.

When I know the way to my destination, I listen to iPod's shuffle. While the robotized voice from a song like Beastie Boys' "Intergalactic Planetary" is unmistakable, other songs' electronic vocals are less discernible. Songs garble. I often misremember the origins of concatenated, vocoded, and autotuned lyrics, accidentally transplant, fuse, and mash them up:

> "You must be a libra. Your place or mine?"[1] I took a cab there,[2] through the night,[3] [to] your place,[1] down the hills,[3] up in the woods,[4] smiling in the back seat,[5] strapped in.[5] Driven into frozen winter,[5] I took a cab[2] [on] an odyssey to pleasure.[7] I [wanted] to drive.[3] I [wanted][3] [a] better driver,[5] a safer car,[5] a car wash.[5] "I'm giving you a[3] good memory[5] [at] your place.[1] I'm giving you[3] pleasure.[7] I want you,[7] I [am] trying to make contact,[8] trying to make[8] kisses with saliva,[5] trying to make[8] pleasure."[7] Fuck mechanic[7] knows how to party.[9] "Are you coming?[10] Are you coming?"[10] Are you?[10] "Do you feel like I do?[11] Do you feel like[11] I'm giving

90

you[3] pleasure?[7] O,[10] you feel like[11] winter?"[13] The cita-aay[9] gets cold.[12] "O,[10] you feel[11] blue?"[13] To my amazement,[14] the things we say are not always the things we feel.[15] It doesn't have to be like this. All we have to do is make sure we keep talking.[16] Talking[16] makes us stronger.[17] Talking[16] makes us[17] feel like I do.[11] I'm giving you a night call.[3] I'm gonna[3] [make] us[17] feel like I do.[11] I'm gonna tell you something you don't want to hear:[3] "I'm blue.[13] I want to[3] cry in public.[5] How could you be so heartless?[18] How could you be so[18] childish?[5] How could you be so cold?"[18] "Do you believe in life after[19] blue?[13] Do you believe in life after[19] it's dark?[3] Do you believe in life after[19] it's empty,[5] frantic,[5] winter?"[5]

---

1 Franz Zappa, "Stick It Out"
2 The Knife, "You Make Me Like Charity"
3 Kavinsky, "Nightcall"
4 Bon Iver, "Woods"
5 Radiohead, "Fitter Happier"
6 Powerman 5000, "The Song of X-51"
7 Röyksopp & Robyn, "Sayit"
8 The Carpenters, "Calling Occupants of Enterprise"
9 2Pac, "California Love"
10 Laurie Anderson, "O Superman"
11 Peter Frampton, "Do You Feel Like We Do?"
12 Dan Deacon, "The Crystal Cat"
13 Eifel 65, "Blue (Da Ba Dee)"
14 ??
15 Death From Above 1979, "Do It!"
16 Pink Floyd, "Keep Talking"
17 Daft Punk, "Harder, Better, Faster, Stronger"
18 Kanye West, "Heartless"
19 Cher, "Believe"

"Check you [sic] email," I text Mom. "I sent you a phonology chart." After she's rehearsed, she calls and I record her recitation on speakerphone, but not before she asks, "Why am I doing this again?"

I hesitate, try to circumvent morbidity, can't. "I guess I just want to save your voice. Like, imagine if you could read bedtime stories to your great-great grandchildren."

"Ooh," she says. "*That's* creepy."

It takes over an hour to assemble a fluid reading of the chorus to Robert Munsch's Love You Forever, the bestselling book my mother used to read to me as a child.

Target: "I'll love you forever."	Target: "I'll like you for always."	Target: "As long as I'm living,"	Target: "my baby you'll be."
Phonemes: /ˈī(-ə)l/ /ˈləv/ /ˈyü/ /fə-ˈrev-ər/	Phonemes: /ˈī(-ə)l/ /ˈlīk/ /ˈyü//fər/ /ˈȯl-wēz/	Phonemes: /əz/ /ˈlȯŋ/ /əz/ /ˈīm/ /ˈlivin/	Phonemes: /ˈmī/ /ˈbā-bē/ /ˈyül/ /ˈbē/
Approx. concatenation: [0.3s pause] [long /i/ + /l/] [0.3s pause] [/l/ + /schwa/ + /v/] [0.3s pause] [/y/ + long /oo/] [0.3s pause] [/f/ + /or/ + short /e/ + /v/ + /ur/] [0.3s pause]	Approx. concatenation: [0.3s pause] [long /i/ + /l/] [0.3s pause] [/l/ + long /i/ + /k/] [0.3s pause] [/y/ + long /oo/] [0.3s pause] [/f/ + /or/] [0.3s pause] [/schwa/ + /l/ + /w/ + long /a/ + /z/] [0.3s pause]	Approx. concatenation: [0.3s pause] [short /a/ + /z/] [0.3s pause] [/l/ + /schwa/ + /ng/] [0.3s pause] [short /a/ + /z/] [0.3s pause] [long /i/ + /m/] [0.3s pause] [/l/ + short/i/ + /v/ + short /i/ + /ng/] [0.3s pause]	Approx. concatenation: [0.3s pause] [/m/ + /i/] [0.3s pause] [/b/ + long /a/ + /b/ + long /e/] [0.3s pause] [/y/ + long /oo/ + /l/] [0.3s pause] [/b/ + long /e/] [0.3s pause]

If the embodied voice transmits *viva voce* (i.e., word of mouth, literally "living-voice"), then how does the disembodied voice transmit? *Stereo voce*? *Mortuus voce*? I imagine Mom's voice calling Descartes' 400-hundred-year-old bluff: "I think; therefore, I am or was."

I know that in this amount of time, I could have just recorded Mom reading the bedtime hit parade: *Love You Forever* and *That's Good! That's Bad!* and *Brown Bear, Brown Bear, What Do You See?* and *Just Go to Bed*. That's not the point, though. I am trying to create a pluripotent file that will preserve Mom in a feat of audio cryonics, its pieces' parts able to be uploaded into a clip directory for text-to-speech programs (now), onto a semi-intelligent natural language user interface (later), and onto an artificial intelligence system that can generate its own code from terrabytes, petabytes, and exabytes of data (way later).

I shuffle the .wav files, and Mom seems to be speaking Czech, or she's just making up words, neologisms like "pablem," "urooth," and "bdsk." Like a child acquiring language or a dementia patient losing it, the sounds—consecutive strings blipping into a mesmeric haze—balk at meaning until, after about five minutes, a few discernible words randomly surface: "sting," "bake," "brine." Later, "harrow," "scoff," "lift."

On a night hike pilgrimage to Vaishno Devi Temple in Katra, India, it is impossible to get lost. After five hours of ascent, the temple of the Trikuta Mountains is near, and thousands of people trekking ahead of me are synched in an aerobic mantra, a spoken substitute for low-oxygen respiration: "…Mataji, Mataji, Mataji, Mataji…" I start to say it myself, unsure of what it means, "M-uh-t-uh j-e." A young Indian student next to me is adrenalized by my joining. He pumps his fist at me. We say it a few more times—"…Mataji, Mataji, Mataji…"—before I ask him.

"What does it mean?"

He smiles and points toward the temple above us. "Vaishno

Devi is the Durga, the holiest goddess."

I nod. I already knew that.

"Mataji means 'Respected mother' or 'Eternal Mother,'" he says. "We say it together because Vaishno Devi is mother of us all."

After this explanation, I nod again and pump *my* fist. As an only child, I can't help but think he is telling me, "And you're our brother!"

As I continue the hike, surrounded by rind-gnawing macaques perched on rocks above me, overweight pilgrims supine on comfy stretchers conveyed by pony, porter, or palanquin, and Jammu-Kashmir policemen at frisking stations waiting to detect contraband, I reconsider the *all* of Dad's song ("We're all alone.") Maybe *all* is not modifying the aloneness, but the *we*. We are, all of us, alone. In Katra, rather than wait for Mother to come home, they move toward her.

Mom's frequencies are collected in .wav files, and I trim at digital silences perpetrated on either side of the sounds, until there's just the bare phoneme: short vowels, long vowels, schwa, consonants (*b-z*), diphthongs (*oi-, ow-, oo-, aw-*), digraphs (*ch-, sh-, th-*), and special cases (*hw* as in whistle and *zh* as in garage). Compressed into a file, "Mom.Phonics.mp3," her voice is encrypted (from *krypte*, "hidden vault"), disembodied. I'm unsure what the next step is in this abiotic cryopreservation of Mom. Maybe I'll take her to the mall some day, buy her a nice outfit before a full-body scan, and purchase a statue of her, 1:1 in 3D, embed an electronic voice box within it, her phonemes on shuffle.

Mom, who got us to D.C. and NYC and Atlantic City, all those 90's summer vacations, was replaced by Karen, who got me to Chicago and New Orleans and Akron ("Make the next right turn onto Doctor Martin Luther King Doctor") for '08, '09, and '10 spring breaks, was replaced by Susan, who got me to Tucson for graduate school and Vegas for the clichéd "hell of it" and now Sacramento. Somewhere, the next voice actor is in a studio recording fifty-plus hours of script and sound strings, waiting to introduce herself to me. It's always a woman waiting to tell me how to get to the next place.

Yes, even Siri will be unceremoniously replaced, dragged to a sound archive, a sonic reliquary, all conversations with her voided by a software update that will come like a thief in the night.

Susan's Twitter handle is @SiriuslySusan.

On July 31st, she tweeted: "Happy b-day roses from my fabulous son, Cam! I love you! @CAM_SANDwich #birthdays #happyLeos"

A fan tweets: "He Siriously loves you! :)"

Cameron tweets: "Love you too Mommalla!"

I wonder if, decades from now—post Susan-as-Siri, post-Siri-as-Apple-assistant, post-Susan even, R.I.P.—Cameron will still plug his antique iPhone 5s into the power adapter to resurrect her on her birthday. Viva Susan the voce, whose phonemes are proto-digi-limbic, the vice versa of technophilia, glass and aluminum that loves you too, forever, likes you for always, as long as she's plugged in, a son of sound you can be.

"Happy Birthday, Mom," he might say.

"It's my birthday?"

"Happy Birthday, Mom."

"It's not really my birthday."

"Happy Birthday, Mom."

"If you say so."

This Taxidermy Will Be Mounted to an Interior Wall

2014-01-21 | 09:55:16 | Tue: Two svelte mammals—spines swooped into commas, eyes covered by their own hind legs—rest in their respective black-and-white video feed frames. Their motionlessness makes it unclear whether or not the Phoenix Zoo's live webcams are working, whether the black-footed ferrets are in fact alive. I squint, draw my nose close to the static animal images: Buffering? Sleeping? Dead? The time display in the corner shows how the seconds add. I zoom. I zoom again. +, +, +. My rapt surveillance eliminates the negative space consumed by substrate and metal lace cage door. My screen is filled with just one low-resolution ferret now. He is unmoving, though at the center of him, the pixels fluctuate as his diaphragm puffs with breath. The slight contraction: this thing's alive.

Despite its inclusion in John James Audubon's posthumously published *The Vivaparous Quadrupeds of North America* (1851), Audubon never actually set his failing eyes upon a live black-footed ferret. His son, John Woodhouse, who had taken over the three-volume mammal project, received a ferret pelt by post. It was a "poor specimen" from a fur-trading post near the headwaters of the Platte River in Wyoming, its carcass stuffed with crushed sagebrush. John Woodhouse's plate depicts the weasel thieving eggs from a river nest.

I am imagining the Audubons, along with their naturalist buddy Reverend John Bachmann. They are in a room, taking turn after patient turn, running their thirty quivering fingers through the pelage, describing the interspersion of fine and coarse hairs "below the ears, under the forearms and belly… the tail… cylindrical, and less voluminous than… the mink."

They are defining the palette: "roots whitish, with a yellowish tinge, broadly tipped with reddish-brown," also rufous, black and white.

Bachman writes, "It is with great pleasure that we introduce this handsome new species." Despite the hearty introduction, it took a quarter-century for a *living* specimen to manifest, leaving skeptics to assume the black-footed ferret was modern mythology.

My fiancée leaves at dawn. I spank the bumper of her Jetta, leaning from the sidewalk curb, cement dividing line. I make my way back into the duplex, take a deep breath before opening the door to a new kind of home. Now, the house is just mine. Driving north, she texts about the Vegas buffet: *You should see the seafood. All the mussels and crab legs…* Eating cotton candy and key lime now. There is even a photo message of her eyes peeking over plumes of loose-spun amaranth sugar. I think maybe it won't be so bad as her digital bytes breadcrumb north, where she will be completing a four-month internship in biological conservation in the Great Basin. I stay in Tucson to watch our ferrets. Alone, I misapprehend them, have fantastical delusions that I'm Dar from the 1982 film *Beastmaster* and the ferrets are my hoodwinking companions.

I live on my hands and knees those first loner days, shimmying after ferrets, replicating the guttural chuckles so as to speak like them, with them—dooking, they call it. It is good fun made more so by generous splashes of scotch into a tumbler. I feel abandoned when they dart into the RV air conditioning hose, where they become invisible rustling phantoms. As with the box of packing peanuts, the hose cultivates natural behaviors. My fiancée wants them to learn to burrow like black-footed ferrets of the wild western prairies.

When they burrow into the hose, I lay prostrate, peeking into the tunnel with my bicycle headlamp shining. My forearms reach after them, but the hose restricts me at the biceps. The ferrets play-nip at my fingers. Ookii, Shiroi, and Muzmuzu are all adjusting to life without Chichi, whose absence has become a spiritual void in the Mabel duplex.

While they scuffle in the hose, I drink another scotch, eventually fall asleep waiting for them to exit. They have an unprecedented six-hour run of the house while I'm passed out. In these first days of my fiancée's internship, I tend to sleep on the wooden floor, splayed on twenty-four square feet of grass turf from Lowe's. The ferrets skitter and dook, leap upon me like Podo and Kodo rousing their beastmaster. I stay zonked until dawn, the Tucson sun hoisting over the Rincon Mountains in the east.

By the early twentieth century, ferret breeding became a lucrative business in the Midwest. In *Ferret Facts and Fancies* (1915), trapper and fur buyer Arthur Harding discusses how a single breeder, Henry Farmsworth, jumpstarted the new industry whose annual weasel sales exceeded the human population of Ferretville, Ohio (also called New London) thirteenfold. Single orders were filled for several hundred ferrets. Aerated crates stocked with limber, musky, dooking ferrets were sold to wharfs, where they hunted the cargo-feeding rats that boarded the ships by mooring ropes. Other ferrets were sold into municipal labor.

In the early 1900s, America had the highest teledensity (number of telephone connections per hundred households) of any country due to, in no small part, black-footed ferrets. Mr. Cline, superintendent of the Central Union Telephone Company of Indianapolis, deployed ferrets throughout communities of central Indiana.

A ferret was "harnessed and muzzled," then sent into ducts, through which it chased a live rat. The ferrets dragged lacing twine by which workmen pulled through a telephone wire. Those first magical telephone calls of the early 1900s were made possible by industrious ferrets that rodded ducts connecting buildings' phone lines.

Several times, while ferretsitting for my fiancée, Ookii went missing in the walls of crappy duplex construction. I called my fiancée to ask what I should do. "Find him," she said obviously. "Check all the holes. If his head fits, his body will too." He vanquished the obstacle course of gypsum board, recessed cabinetry, fiberglass insulation, electrical wires, and plumbing. As I searched for him on my hands and knees, ringing bells to lure him back, I knew he was found as my neighbors shrieked. He had managed to burrow from a small hole in our bathroom to an even smaller hole in my neighbors' kitchen. They thought he was a mutant rat. I collected him at the threshold—his lank bodice sooty, convulsing with sneezes—and bathed him. I called my fiancée and told her I found him. "Good," she said.

Our domestic ferrets snooze most of the day in handmade, hand-sewn holiday-themed hammocks. We go to Jo-Ann Fabrics, and I choose a few motifs—holly (December), Steelers (January), Cupids (February), then shamrocks. I carry the fabric, and jolly Jo-Ann workers cut it, asking, "Do you have a special project in mind?"

While my fiancée is in the Great Basin, in Nevada's Nye County, the ferrets restlessly scratch at their shamrock hammock as if digging up clover. The sewing machine is in the closet. I call my fiancée from Jo-Ann's, hoping to connect. I have forgotten if it's supposed to be a half-yard or full yard of fabric. I will have a motif ready for her when she visits home. She doesn't pick up.

On cell phone coverage maps, Nevada is among the least speckled states. There, the dead zones stretch on for miles. The cell phone searches and searches for signal. Due to its remoteness, the Great Basin was the last explored region in the contiguous United States. Unsurprisingly, Nye County is home to the largest zero-population tract of the 2000 United States Census.

I buy pastel egg (April) and margarita (May) motifs. Jo-Ann's is a lonely place when you're on your own. Ambitious grandmothers collect materials for quilts, afghans, or grandkids' costumes with strict dress rehearsal deadlines. I see their arthritic hands clutch at the fabric and watch them shuffle behind carts. I can't help the morbid worries that their projects will go unfinished.

My only trip to Nye County, Nevada was to the Nevada National Security Site, formerly the Nevada Testing Site or Nevada Proving Grounds, the Department of Defense operation home to Yucca Flat. According to author Gerard Clarfield, it is "the most irradiated, nuclear-blasted spot on Earth." In the nuclear era, this desert stretch of Nye County was famous for its kiloton crater pocks and miles-high mushroom-tipped pillars of smoke. When her voice crinkles due to bad reception, I imagine it's the waves of radiation absorbing our conversation. My ears squint to hear her voice. "I think we're breaking up again," I tell her before the call is dropped.

During one rare late-March phone call, my fiancée wants me to put her on speakerphone, to put her voice next to the ferrets' cage. I rouse them from their recently shampooed hammocks, and they sniff at the sound of her voice with their coffee bean noses. The call is dropped before the receiver returns to my ear.

The first ferret arrived in North America during the Pleistocene ice ages, emigrating from Siberia over a grassland steppe, the erstwhile Beringia. It was a robust species, slinking at the ankles of woolly mammoths, lions, horses, and camels. The oldest fossil specimen—at least 750,000 years old—was found in Cathedral Cave, Nevada and elucidates the evolutionary history of the species.

Over the course of the twentieth century, the black-footed ferret became a relict organism, its populations diminished due to sylvatic plague, canine distemper, the American Fur Company, and the eradication of the prairie dog (essentially the ferret's sole menu item). In 1967, ferrets were included on the first-ever Endangered Species List.

According to conservationist Denny Hammer in a video for the Wyoming Game and Fish Department, "in 1972, a black-footed ferret was found dead in a stock tank near Leo, Wyoming, and that was the last… evidence that possibly they still existed." This ferret was found in the Shirley Basin, just 650 miles away from the Nevadan fossil prototype. "And then, about 1979," Hammer said, "most people felt that black-footed ferrets were extinct… until…"

On September 26, 1981, a Saturday morning, after having breakfast with his wife Lucille, maybe a chicken fried steak like she cooked at Lucille's Café on weekdays on State Street in downtown Meeteetse, ranch owner John Hogg opened the front door of his house in the hopes of finding his ranch dog, a blue-heeler named Shep, who was last seen scuffling the evening before (with a presumed porcupine), and after looking out at the distant foothills of the Absaroka Range of Northwest Wyoming near Yellowstone's perimeter, and then at the gap filled by rolling shortgrass prairie, chutes of blue grama covering the Hogg and Pitchfork ranches, and then at the near lawn where Shep usually loped but was hitherto absent, and eventually at the ground immediately at his feet, where an animal—willowy with champagne fur, splotches of sable and soot, its skull blunt, adorned with two triangular ears, teeny-legged and long-tailed—an offering to the family from Shep, laid supine and stiff, John went to his knees. Having never seen such a thing in his life, he inspected the carcass closely.

In John Hogg's own words: "I stepped out there and looked… there was this ferret… I didn't know it was a ferret. It was laying on the ground. I looked at it and pretty soon, well, I picked it up, brought it in, laid it down, showed it to Lucille." Lucille encouraged John to take it to town to be mounted. The taxidermist Larry LaFranchi watched in disbelief as John dumped the small mammal from the gunnysack onto the floor. Like the Audubons over 130 years earlier, the two were stupefied by it. LaFranchi took it to the back and made a phone call, and John Hogg "never had a say about whether [he] was gonna get it back or not."

David Cunningham, Director of the Meeteetse Museum,

describes what followed as "an onslaught of biologists, wildlife experts, and press." In another interview, Hogg unceremoniously said if he had known how that ferret would disrupt the town, he would have just chucked the body over his fence.

After Chichi died, my fiancée began searching for internships in New Mexico, California, Nevada, Wyoming, and Montana, saying each state name as if it was only a county away. She wanted to work with small mammals, to conserve as many as she could after losing just her one.

Her internship in the Great Basin—in service to all the pocket mice, kangaroo mice, harvest mice, bushy-tailed woodrats, desert woodrats, deer mice, canyon mice, Pinyon mice, and grasshopper mice—turns her nocturnal. My days begin just as hers end. In that languorous hour, we're both barely awake, not wanting to contend with the static. Once, she gets a ride into town, goes to Kozy Korner for WiFi, where she tells me about Tonopah's silver mining history, the ancient bristlecone pine forest, the Clown Motel, and the man with the full-body cat tattoo from Guinness World Book. All the catch up gives me whiplash.

She works at night when the small mammals are out and about. The only exception, she says, is during the full moon phase when small nocturnal animals reduce travel to avoid risk of predation. Max illumination means visibility, risk. For kit foxes, it's like floodlights on prey. "I can come home then," she volunteers. *When the mice are burrowed.* "Think about it." She says goodbye, and the absolute silence recommences.

I start to watch the moon as lunar time signature. I mark the potential return dates on a calendar

*2012-04-06	19:19**	*Homecoming?*
*05-06	03:35*	*Homecoming?*
*06-04	11:12*	*Homecoming?*
*07-03	18:52*	*Homecoming?*

*Full moon times according to National Oceanic and Atmospheric Administration (NOAA)

Sitting on a lawn chair near my backyard fire pit, scotch-sipping again, I dare myself to ignore the moon, to stop time. I've been spending more and more time poolside, away from the adobe walls, inside which feels more like a burrow network than a duplex. When the fire smolders, I sway through the door, enter the bedroom, and say to the bed, "I don't want to sleep on you anymore." I make the bed inoperable, stripping the bedclothes, a Serta tabula rasa. I flop the mattress off the box spring, lean it against the window, crushing the PVC blinds.

Staring at myself in the mirror, I call it like I see it: "You drunk."

I sit on the floor and extract small threads of cactus from my foot and ankle with tweezers and drop the spines into my empty tumbler. The white ferret with the red eyes scurries beneath the bedframe. Small beads of blood stipple my heel.

I bait Shiro and scoop him from the floor. We do pirouettes into the kitchen, but when his eyes dilate, I set him down. He does weasel plyometrics to escape me. I collapse on the green turf and call for another ferret. "Chichi!" I call. "Cheech!" I forget he's dead.[1]

I move on to the others, bellowing a mock roll call: Ookii, Shiroi, Muzumuzu. I cry in my weasel falsetto "here" after each name. Then, I call my fiancée's name and let silence testify.

I am cheered thinking of all the small mammals reunited in

[1] Chichi, not quite short for Chisai, meaning small in Japanese. Always chasing after the others, especially Ookii, meaning big. Little chasing big. Not tonight. *Not being himself*. Chichi, we call Cheech Marin, Tsichi Fly, Chi Wee or Chi Weasel, Parcheezy and Young Weezy. Our smallest ferret is *dragging, not being himself*. Chichi, also known as Cheeto Magito and Pezhead as when he looks at the world upside down. Chichi, runty and deaf. We sometimes wrestle too hard. Chichi, precious plaything, your ears are ornamental. They say he can feel vibrations. I recline him on the bridge of a guitar, pluck strings until he tries crawling into the hole to get at the heart of sound. His whiskers dust the rosette inlay. The wee one with the white knees, the Waardenburg weasel. He is cold, nose and gums pale. Look at him and wonder. Hammock the other two. Los tres amigos are minus one. The Apt. B qì is off, life-force unflowing. Swaddle Cheech in the blanket and go. We are without GPS, and the way is unknown. We U-turn, brake, right turn, maybe wrong turn, curb-crawl until we've found the emergency pet center. Chichi, we

their burrows during the full moon phase, nestled against one other. Mischiefs of mice, the nuclear (small mammal) families of the Great Basin. More cheered for them, I think, than I am for my own reunion. *Homecoming?* is anon. I drink more scotch, maybe without rinsing away the cactus spines.

In Scott Weidensaul's *The Ghost with Trembling Wings* (2002), he calls the black-footed ferret a "[phantom]: secretive, highly nocturnal, almost entirely subterranean… A prairie dog town is the ferret's universe," he says. It is a "shelter, larder, birthing chamber, and tomb, all in one." With John Hogg's permission, Denny Hammer and other conservationists explored the ranch, surveying the prairie dog towns, hoping to find clues that a live "business" of ferrets was burrowed beneath the ranch.

Thirty-three days after LaFranchi called the Wyoming Game and Fish Department from his taxidermy office, Denny Hammer and a partner arrived. After driving the ranch roads for days, they spotted the first live ferret at 6:20 a.m. It ran alongside

also call Chimney or Chi-ma-ny, Chi Money and Chisus: little savior. Not perfect, nor innocent. Nebshit and wirechew. Though secretly favorite: count the many utterances of his name, each born of a different brand of love. Chichi is in the clinic. My fiancée is more devoted to the species than I am. There is a possibility of an enlarged and ruptured spleen. Restless. Waiting. We should have brought his things on strings: loofa and the belled Indian elephants. Strange talismans. On his island with just three favorite things, these would be there. My fiancée too. She cannot imagine a world without ferrets. In the clinic without her *Princeton Encyclopedia of Mammals*, she rewraps a cold bundle of two pounds, one ounce. In the field, she begins with density maps and radio telemetry. But Chichi is right here, everywhere to be found, consciousness flickering. We sing his name to "Rocket Man," "Dreamweaver," "Tiny Dancer," "Notorious," and that one song by the Ting Tings. Calling all love and support: Chichi is in the clinic. Honorary godmothers of Gage Street, pray. This pitiful thing. The way he clinches fingers with his curling paws, dexterous monkeyman. In critical condition now, it will cost to stabilize him. We're talking plasma donations again, our desperation ATM. Later, I'll look for things to blame. Magellan GPS as murderer. Marshall's as murderer. Duk Soup as murderer. Me as murderer. (We sometimes wrestle too hard.) The surgery is "exploratory," and we haven't got the money. I am grunting at the itemized estimate, insulted by $87 for surgical prep, for shaving fur from crotch and abdomen. We tell ourselves, tell Chichi that not having the money for him is different than not having the love. Chisai, meaning small, but whose life was big. We loved. Chichi, secretly chimera, a ferret for sure but with something limbic about you we've detected. *They called him Chichi. They called him Chi. That was his name. That was his name!*

the conservationists' pickup truck. Hammer, on the passenger side, watched it scurry away to a nearby hole. He and his partner followed, and the ferret taunted them from the opening, only half-submerged. Hammer recalled that first sustained glimpse: "The picture of his face, the black mask, the Mickey Mouse kind of ears and the little spots over the eyes. We saw everything… we needed to see."

Because prairie dog burrows have multiple points of ingress and egress, the conservationists plugged all holes associated with the system, trapping ferret "620." Hammer sat in a lawn chair wrapped in tarp. It was a frigid twenty degrees, and the ferret was shallow in the trap, not stepping far enough to engage the treadle. When 620 was finally captured, he was taken back to camp to endure surveillance.

From Hammer's ecstatic field journals:

0600: Leave camp with b-f-f to release back at the Pitchfork Ranch… The ferret appears to be in good condition, got restless during the night, but always settled back down. Barked at me this morning. 0627: Arrive at Pitchfork Ranch. 0636: Arrive at trap site. 26 exposures on my camera. 0645: Attempted the release but antelope hunters detained us. Temperature about thirty degrees. 620… left the box. Hesitated for two to five minutes and then ran down the road about thirty yards and ran into a single entrance mound. Twenty-seven minutes later, he came up and ran to another, has been repeating this sequence of events ever since. 0830: He's been down below ground for about twenty-six minutes. No one before has ever done what we have just completed in the last day and half: located, trapped, radioed and released a b-f-f. Also at 0705, a golden eagle flew over 620, but didn't attempt to take him. 0930: We lost the signal.

Meeteetse, a Siouxan word meaning "meeting place," was the last-ever meeting place for wild black-footed ferrets in the United States. Over 128 black-footed ferrets (one-third of Meeteetse's human population) were caught-and-released thanks to

620's lead. The business was monitored for months, but was eventually infected by the canine distemper virus. The Wyoming Game and Fish Department developed a recovery plan, including a captive breeding program. The seventeen captive specimens were representatives of one of the rarest mammal species on earth. In the September 9th, 1986 edition of the *Meeteetse Herald*, the boldfaced headline read: "All ferrets captured." The last wild-born black-footed ferret, a single holdout, was discovered in February, and joined the others in Laramie. To this day, all living ferrets—from Alberta, Canada to Chihuahua, Mexico—are believed to be descendants of the original Meeteetse business.

2013-12-26 | 01:03:36 | Th: Two ferrets rarely inhabit the same frame. Because ferrets are fossorial, they often hide out of sight of the infrared cameras in the black plastic tubes at the Phoenix Zoo. I monitor the housing like it's a screensaver. According to Paula Swanson, who manages the ferrets, the enclosures are 48"x 36"x 24" with sealed plywood floor and sealed wooden frames. There is plastic-coated mesh wire and ventilated nest boxes accessible by 4"-wide corrugated black plastic tubing. The nest boxes are divided into a sleeping area with soft paper-based bedding and a latrine area. Occasionally, there are enrichment items such as paper bags, paper towel tubes, and golf balls to incite hunting instincts. I envision our duplex miniaturized, to-scale with the ferret enclosures, an adobe dollhouse. How much of me could fit inside?

I sleep out of my bed for 78 of 81 nights—stick to the floor, my desk, patio furniture, and even dry riverbeds when I don't feel like driving drunk. There is implicit real estate in Tucson's Rillito River drainage pipes. The most coveted spots are beneath the Catalina No. 7 housing development on River Road, a gated community with password-protected keypads. There are hostile homeless who command me to turn around, do not try to pass through, turn off the headlamp, *fuck* and *Christ* and *asshole*. I romantically think that they might guru me, teach me what it means to be displaced, but being among them makes me understand less. Unlike me, they did not choose to leave home. From scant conversation, I glean it was joblessness leading to mortgage delinquency; disorder leading to delusion or paranoia; alcoholism or drug use leading to severance from family. Several are veterans. I pay April's rent, but it feels more like a storage fee. I return home only long enough to feed the ferrets.

The homeless burrow in the pipes, sleeping soundly beneath four-bedroom houses with vacant guest bedrooms. The pipes are littered with hospital bracelets, aluminum, glass, candy wrappers, condom boxes, and swatches of tarpaulin. Where do they go when monsoon comes, when the river actually rivers? Do they get washed out of their pipe homes, punched out by hydropower and gravity, spat into the desert by the gush of the artificial flume?

My feet dangle from the Rillito River walking path, heels butting against the bank. The underside of the bridge erupts in a whispery squeaky fuss. Mexican free-tailed bats sweep from the bridge's extension joints. They swarm into a vortex. The green-thumb grandmas scrape away the skunky-smelling bat guano into plastic pails for composting. They wear shredded scarves to keep from inhaling the bat shit's fungal spores. The quiet *squee-squee* is replaced by horses' whinnying, ATVs' revving, a congregation at the bridge. Finally, one bat flies tangential to the vortex's curve. The rest follow into twilight.

One bat plops dead on the asphalt walking trail, fallen from its perch. A little boy in striped overalls flips it over with an ocotillo poker. With the poker tucked under the elastic of the wings, the bat does dead somersaults to the bank's brink, twelve grams of fuzz and ornamental bones turned over and over until it disappears into the wash with the abysmal clatter of gravel. I ask myself what-if questions about my fiancée's internship applications. What if she had stuck with the Tucson bat internship instead of the Reno mice? What if she had elected to stay instead of go? The bats stream westward away from the maternity colony to feast on the suburb's moth buffet.

My fiancée enters the house on Mabel Street. I ask why she didn't knock, and she reminds me that she lives here with me, that her name is still on the lease. She says this delicately, speaking to me as if I'm an amnesiac. I realize that if I prefer her to knock, then she has rapidly blurred into a stranger.

Her stay is brief, our interactions routine. Mostly, we play with ferrets.

The night before she has to go back, her spine is torqued against mine in bed. I stare at the highway map of the United States on the wall. Tucson is six inches from the Great Basin, the distance slight with the distortion of scale, the same as the canyon between our vertebrae. The legend explains how a single inch can be a hundred miles.

We had pressed glittery star stickers all over the map to commemorate the trips we had taken over the years. Insomnious, I try to trace our cumulative vector path, from first sticker (Pittsburgh) to last. Pittsburgh. Akron. Cleveland. Columbus. Buffalo. Toronto. Detroit. Cadillac. New York City. Philadelphia. Dover. Lewes. Rehoboth. Las Vegas. The stars pulse with my perception. Ocean City. Washington D.C. Williamsburg. Baltimore. Nashville. Memphis. Montgomery. The sticker stars twinkle then burst. New Orleans. Baton Rouge. Orlando. Kissimmee. Chicago. Tucson. I am chasing after the most recent star, where our bittersweet trajectory splices. Boston. Salem. Indianapolis. Saint Louis. Oklahoma City. El Paso. Phoenix. Sedona. Dallas. Greenville. Spartanburg. Little Rock. Austin. San Diego. Flagstaff. Grand Canyon. The last is Seligman. South of the Grand Canyon, I had to stencil Seligman onto the map, estimate its geography.

Just before her Nevadan internship, I went with my fiancée to Seligman in Northern Arizona to spotlight for the real deal black-footed ferrets. The Aubrey Valley site is the fourth successful reintroduction site of the black-footed ferret conservation effort, abundant with Meeteetse's *mustela nigripes* progeny. According to the Arizona Game and Fish Department, the goal is to have a "free-ranging, self-sustaining population of black-footed ferrets." By transecting through prairie dog towns with GPS, conservationists can count and record burrow activity and generate density maps of habitats.

On the first night, we drove to our assigned transect and entered through the iron orange gates of the host ranch. We drove dirt roads designed for tractors, occasionally braking for stubborn bovine crossing the road. The SUV idled slowly as we took turns holding wheel then spotlight. My fiancée aimed the light from her passenger window. The first ferret's eyes reflected emerald green as ten million candlepower illuminated the *tapetum lucidem* eye shine. As the emeralds bounced across the ranch earth, we parked, took the small mammal traps from the back hatch of the SUV, plugging the burrow holes with traps capped with burlap sacks to simulate burrow continuation. We recorded GPS longitude and latitude and left, invigorated to discover more emeralds. By the time we returned to the first site, the ferret had stomped the treadle, trapping himself.

We carried the trap to the car, where he barked ferociously in the backseat. We took private peeks at him while driving to the RV. Inside, we watched our ferret wince as he was anesthetized, then injected with a passive integrated transponder (PIT) tag. The PIT tag meant there was no previous record of this ferret, making him—in that instant—the newest triumph of the conservation effort. The conservationists inoculated him for canine distemper and administered a penicillin booster.

When the research technician asked what we wanted to name him, we thought of our domestic ferrets at home—Ookii, Muzumuzu, and Shiroi—and decided on homage to the late Chisai. Chichi Too, we called him. My fiancée held him as I took a photo. When he awoke, he was fed prairie dog meat, and the blood dripped from his jowls. We returned him to his home burrow. My fiancée waited in the heated car while I crunched across the frost, swinging open the cage door at the burrow ingress.

The ferret waited to see what I'd do next. I stood stock still until he disappeared into the earth.

I have a recurring dream in which all my ex-lovers live on a desert island—and not just them, but non-lovers too. The ones who knew I could love them but wouldn't let me. The ones whose names I bubbled onto burnt CD-Rs. The ones I knew only by their cryptic initials or screen names. The island is similar to Gilligan's, though occasionally it's an urban condominium with tropical décor. I call it Ex Isle. I admit that, the first couple times, in the lucid secrecy of fantasy, I willed it to be a harem.

Instead, they live communally, refusing to speak to me. They aren't ignoring me to be spiteful. They just know that I have nothing left to offer them, that I've already lavished all my energies upon them, that the one they loved (that version of me) is extinct. They have tabulated, in joules, the disparate expenditures between the ceremony of our first date and the faint tremors of our last encounter. They know I'm depleted, so they've become self-reliant. It's a strange dream because it does not try to counterfeit reality. They know I'm visiting from my reality, vacationing back to them for a paranoid audit of my past. The dream is a neurotic roll call.

I overhear DJ say my fiancée's name to one of the other women.

"You know her?" I ask, but I'm ignored. "How do you know her? Is she on this island now too?"

Nobody responds, but I know the answer. My bio TA reclines in a hammock between two palm trees. The fabric is classic Jo-Ann's.

In the morning before she leaves, I cup my fiancée's hand, rotate the engagement ring on her finger in a half-revolution.

"Has your finger gotten smaller?" I ask.

She isn't sure.

"Thanks for coming," I say, but it doesn't sound earnest. I know.

She says goodbye to her ferrets for over an hour: to Ookii, to Shiroi, to Muzumuzu. It culminates with her scooping them into a ferret Cerberus, kissing each wet nose one by one. She attends to me in her last few minutes.

"Are you actually going to throw those away?" she asks, gesturing to the scotch bottles conglomerated on the counter. I nod. We share a small hug goodbye. We're wordless, unsure of what comes next. Back inside the house, at 7 a.m., I splash scotch into a tumbler for my first on the rocks.

Fiancée: The new moon is the dark moon. You're not coming, but going, going, gone. Now firmly elsewhere. I strip the mattress, stand it up. Where in the land are you now, fiancée-cum-biotechnician? I fold up the wall map, wish I could fold up these walls too. The new moon is the luna tabula rasa. Mammals abound under dark desert sky: you have work to do. If when the moon waned full, you conversed, waxing now, you conserve.

When in dark tunnels—whether interior walls, municipal manholes, or wild prairie dog burrows—ferrets are likely to take unannounced siestas. Their nocturnal nature and frequent sleep patterns make them inefficient candidates for twenty-first century broadband distribution, though according to *The Telegraph*, they are still occupied by Virgin Media in more rural areas.

In June, I send my fiancée a text about deposit slips before shutting off my phone for a week. I deactivate my Facebook account, wondering why social media has failed to salve our long distance wounds. I pretend our long-distance learning curve has been technological and not limbic.

Imaginary source code for deactivating a Facebook account:

```
deactivate::{["Engaged_to_the_[sic]Technician"]}...
{"resources":["yxq3J","HwjeW"]}..."legacy:ajaxpipe"...ASync...
deactivate::{["Evade_chatter_of,_photos_of,_shared_links_of,_false_
friends_who,_mind-numbing_ennui."]},"..."legacy:Toggler"
```

After our first night of ferret spotlighting in Seligman, we escaped the Aubrey Cliffs at dawn. At the rusting historical sign, "birthplace of Route 66," I set my camera's timer and sprinted to the side opposite my fiancée. We waited for the flash bulb to be snapshotted with this emblem of long distance. At the Roadkill Café, we discussed her internship options, both crossing fingers for the Tucson bat internship.

In the Elvis Room at the Canyon Lodge, I scanned all the Elvis portraits and memorabilia. "We should have gone to Graceland when we were in Memphis," I said. She mildly agreed, but was distracted by transect maps. I tested her commitment to our engagement: "We should have had Elvis marry us at the Little White Chapel when we were in Vegas." She looked up from her maps and rolled her eyes. At the kitsch? At actually reaching our engagement's finish line? At the profane combination of the two?

I continued eyeing the Elvis photos. My fiancée muttered something about Elvis taxa, impersonator species, Lazarus taxa, zombie species, distinct morphologies, a lexicon that's since disintegrated in my memory.

2014-01-07 | 23:09:05 | Tue: I sneak up on the computer screen, watch the Phoenix Zoo's live web cam, feeling as if I'm in the ferret enclosure. One goes through a tube, ends up in a different frame. One climbs the cage. Now, there are four ferrets. A ferret poops, and his comrade takes a faithful whiff. This is what revival looks like. They are oblivious to their celebrity, ignorant of the re-extinction chatter, unaware of the brink they traverse.

In July, my fiancée leaves for good. She will begin her master's in Florida, leave me to mine in Tucson. (To Be Dumped) She leaves her yellow diamond ring. I keep it in a Zip Loc in a drawer of my nightstand, write *TBD* in Sharpie. (To Be Determined (later)) (To Be Determined (resolved)) State law calls the ring a "conditional gift." (To Be Dissolved) She takes her ferrets with her, and when I ask to say goodbye, she hoists the cage. "Say it," she says. I go to my knees and look at each of them through the metal cage door (To Be Detained), their broaching whiskers.

I wander stuporously to the JFK martini bar, a buttery foot-hill dinner, and end at the batty river wash. It's the beginning of a month-long loop, swallowing over a thousand dollars on the rocks (To Be Drunk), becoming unaccountable, whispering scotch to bartenders, the sound like a hyperextended ellipsis, an affectless request. I have a delusion that top shelf will slow me down, but it doesn't. (To Be Delusional)

"Lagavulin Laphroaig Laphroaig Lagavulin Laphroaig Lagavulin Laphroaig"

(To Be Dumb)
(To Be Dizzy)
(To Be Doomed)
(To Be Destructible)
(To Be Destroyed)
(To Be Damned)
(To Be Done (for))
(To Be Deliverable (from evil))
(To Be Done (finished))

Years later, I write an email to conservationists in Seligman *(Maybe this is an asinine request, but can you tell me: do you know if Chichi Too is still jouncing around the Aubrey Cliffs? Has he been re-captured recently?)*, but receive no reply.

2014-03-03 | 02:14:26 | Mon: No ferrets today. Sometimes, for various reasons, they are quarantined. Even in captivity with constant monitoring, the species remains fragile. Some frank conservationists predict that the species will dwindle again. The *mustela nigripes* conservation battle is a precipitously uphill one.

I can't tell whether the enclosure looks smaller or larger without its residents keeping scale. I have decided that only my disembodied head would actually fit inside the cage. I imagine it inhaling, blinking, and sneezing at the residual musk. My head waits for the ferrets to return post-quarantine. They slink around it, hurdle over it, burrow within it, further within.

Elegy for a Flushed or Buried Pet

For $125 dollars, I could keep the chameleon. Often, keeping a pet and keeping a pet alive are identical enterprises: maintain habitat, provide diet, and remove waste. Fraternity optional.

Can we keep it? Possession. Can we keep it (alive)? Can we keep it (alive (and well)), turn this screen terrarium into something hallowed, corkscrew the scandent stems to confuse his containment, juke the limits until he's maybe in Malagasy terroir: steppe substrate (PetSmart's ReptiBark), savannah turf tiles (Lowe's polypropylene), jungle vine (Jo-Ann's vinyl).

Unlike the Leopard Gecko and Fire-Bellied Newt and Oregon Newt and Green Tree Frog and Asian Greenback Frog and Water Dragon and even the two Figure-Eight Spotted Puffers (Byron and Leroy) whose brackish pH was always in flux (I shook salt into their tank every morning), the chameleon was the only "Intermediate" pet I had ever owned, its care more involved than the others.

I spent hours hovering over Chaleido's body, waiting for the comically long tongue to nab the crickets I'd powdered and delivered to him. I often missed it, though, too distracted by his casque veil, zygodactyl mittens, and stereoscopic cockle eyes. When inside the cage, Chaleido gripped the vine spray. Outside, he maneuvered along the angular sculpture I made from my non-punk tee coat hangers, super-glued to resemble the structure of M. C. Escher's *House of Stairs*. The six-legged, human-footed, parrot-beaked, stalk-eyed creature that climbs Escher's famous stairs (taxonomically: *Pedalternorotandomovens centroculatus articulosus*, colloquially: *wentelteefje*) still seems more morphologically probable to me than the chameleon. Once, I forgot to zip the cage shut, and I returned home to find Chaleido's mint body on the moss carpet, paws paused on the topmost step, a fond anomaly.

The chameleon—earth+lion (*chthon+leon*)—is a species endemic to Madagascar. According to Bantu mythology, Unkulunkulu ("the very great one") sent a chameleon and a gecko to human-kind with opposing messages.

> Chameleon: Let men not die!
> Gecko: Let men die!

Because the chameleon "loitered in the way," lollygagging on bush fruit, it arrived after gecko. The chameleon's detainment meant Malagasy mortality.

In mortal Madagascar, Famadihana ("the turning of the bones") is a custom in which the Malagasy people un-inter their dead—exhume, wash, dress, and perfume the corpses. It is a chance to dance and whisper new secrets to loved ones before burying them again. *Until next time.*

My last living grandparent was Grandma Bingo. Dad converted a space for her in the dining room directly beneath my bedroom. Dad took care of Grandma Bingo—feeding her, bathing her, and cleaning her waste from the folding commode next to her bed. Because she was his responsibility, I sometimes forgot to visit with her. At 7:15 PM on weekdays, she snapped on the radio, spooled it to full volume, and the rosary's drone gusted through the ventilation to my room. Occasionally, I would join in for just the Fifth Mystery and the Salve Regina, and she flashed her gums at me as we synchronized: "O Clement, O Loving, O Sweet…"

When Grandma Bingo turned off the radio, she claimed to still hear it. "Come listen," she insisted, night after night. For a few, I confirmed. I didn't want to confuse her tinnitus for stupidity. "Come listen," she insisted, and eventually, I took the radio in my hand, tilted it as if to spill out the residual sound before redundantly clicking it (again) to the *off* position. "Come listen," she insisted still, and I'd huddle next to her and close my eyes as if the silence was suddenly acute. Annoyed, Dad resolved to confiscate the radio until the next day's rosary. Even then, her secret circuitry echoed and echoed.

Typically, though, I would not join her. I disregarded the rosary, turned up whatever CD I was listening to in my room—almost always Misfits or Descendents or NOFX—and the common vent between our rooms reverberated secular and non-secular non-sequiturs: "I want to be masochistic. / I want to be a statistic… that we may be made worthy… playing with a grin, singing gibberish… I believe in the holy… the holy…" I was a devotee to the bratty logic of punk, the profundity of Fat Mike's oblique antimetaboles: "There's something grand about being nothing / there's something lame about being grand…"

For the first thirteen years, my temperament was ideal for the "Beginner" parent; Dad's biggest challenge was to convince me to bat left-handed in Little League. This changed suddenly when I found a stockpile of punk abandoned in the CD Extreme parking lot along Route 30. The sloppy aesthetic of punk was barely listenable, yet I couldn't stop listening, an oxymoronic sound barrier that suggested "KEEP AWAY FROM THIS BEDROOM." I cut grass, mulched, and weeded, saving my summer funds for pets and punk: Pennywise, newt, Anti-Flag, water dragon, Operation Ivy, puffer fish. Pets swung in the ventilated cardboard boxes and discs bounced in my oversized cargo pockets, awaiting next rotation on the Discman. By 2006, I had filled two 120-disc towers with punk.

I owned just one vinyl record, though I had no way of playing it. I hid the 12" of NOFX's *Heavy Petting Zoo* under the bed. Whereas the CD cover featured a Charlie Sheen-looking cartoon molesting a sheep, fondling its breasts and genitals on an otherwise idyllic farm, the vinyl cover intensified the perversity: the same Sheenish cartoon's face buried between wool thighs, foreshanks flailing in mid-air while the lamb inversely muzzles the man's genitals. In *Screaming for Change: Articulating a Unifying Philosophy of Punk Rock,* Lars J. Kristiansen analyzes the image, "Eating Lamb":

> The fact that none of the songs on [*Heavy Petting Zoo*] deal with animals, zoos, or even bestiality, supports the assertion that the artwork contains little, if any, significant meaning other than portraying images the band is confident will upset and shock the establishment. (113)

Zoophilia is a recurring barb of punk culture, from the deranged Canadian thrashcore band Dayglo Abortions ("the [hamsters] all have Habitrail tubes stuck firmly up their asses / each hamster has an orgasm at the very instant of its death") to the tiresome juvenilia of Blink-182 ("I want to fuck a dog in the ass... I tried to fuck your mom in the ass / tried to fuck your dad in the ass / but could only find the dog, and his ass"). Even mild-mannered Belle and Sebastian's debut album *Tigermilk* (also from 1996) has a cover depicting a lactating mother sitting in the bathtub while a species-ambiguous infant suckles. The faceless baby wears a tiger costume, its ears cockeyed, and it's unclear if it's meant to be an erotic moment, or simply intimate. I looked to the antechambers of my bedroom, the half-dozen cages encaging and decided the doors and lids and zippers were all designed to temper the connection between the keeper and his keep.

When the Grandma-Son din was too much and Dad struggled to concentrate on the local sports news network, he pounded a closed fist against my door and sanctioned me to rosary recitation.

Afterward, Grandma Bingo would ask, "Where's that *thing*?" Sitting upright in bed, she leaned her bony back against the plaster wall, wearing thermal shirts that I outgrew in middle school.

"Upstairs," I'd say. "Do you want me to go get him?"
She smiled without teeth, a slow gummy arc that was gradually becoming familiar to me.
Yes. I brought Chaleido to her, and she opened her usual line of inquiry.

"What's it called?"
"Chameleon," I said.
chthon+leon

What's it called?
I call it my habit—to accumulate and keep, to keep and keep alive.

"Where does it come from?"
"The pet store," I said.
Malagasy terroir

Where does it come from?
A fear that if I am first to encounter the corpse, I will begin resuscitating and not know when to stop. That I will not know when to forfeit the breath. Would I just kiss death, and kiss it again? One breath too many is necromancy.

"What's it do?"
"Just this," I said, hoisting him eye-level. Stereoscopic, he sees us both.
It loiters in the way.

What's it do?
Keeping things alive keeps me alive. Words especially so. A rune

for every soundwave.

"How much did it cost?" This was her favorite question to ask. She scanned the frivolous pet whose hands clung to mine.
"Fifty dollars," I'd lie. Even still, she'd be outraged. I shrunk the price tag over the weeks, but could never find one of which she approved.
For $125, I could keep the chameleon.

How much did it cost?
Indeed.

Sometimes, I showed her the crickets too.
"Is that JELL-O?" she asked.
The crickets perched like gargoyles on the gelatinous heap of Fluker's Cricket Quencher. I shook my head.

A cricket stridulates when it rubs its smooth leathery wing over its toothed wing. According to Robillard and Montealegre, as the cricket stridulates, it "holds the wings up and open, so that the wing membranes can act as acoustical sails," amplifying the chirp.

In early December, a cricket escaped the grip of my forceps, flinging itself away from Chaleido's terrarium, hopping then diving into the dark ducts that connected my room with Grandma's.

Grandma Bingo's rosary delusions were replaced by cricket treble. She wondered how it stayed alive in the furnace's blastway. I'd learned the previous year from a senior prank (dozens of large crickets freed into the dropped ceiling of the high school in balmy May) that crickets chirp more rapidly in warmer temperatures.

The cricket stayed burrowed in the duct, chirping, taunting Chaleido and the other lizards. Recall Stephen King's screenplay for

Pet Sematary (1989), which begins:

FADE IN ON

That most persistent summer SOUND: crickets in high grass—
Ree-ree-ree-ree… This in dark which slowly
                              DISSOLVES TO:
EXT.   A GRAVE MARKER   SUMMER DAY

I'd set Chaleido on Grandma Bingo's robe (mint on royal blue),
and he'd enter the rosary's loop like a jump rope. I'd kneel on the
ground, ear to vent, eyes closed, listening: the hopeless cricket
stridulated like a squeaky film reel, a jammed caster, a hopping
sparrow. How many thousands of crickets I kept cooped and
how many hundreds died before the coming of the forcep se-
lector. How many I whisked to the toilet as I choked on the
cloying odor of their spoiled carcasses. Yet only one became a
pet of sorts. For weeks, it stayed stridulent; but just as the sound
became commonplace, it went silent.

"I guess it died," Grandma Bingo shrugged. I half-expected for
her to hear its phantom notes, but she who pored over daily
obituaries—in Gazette and Tribune—knew better than to hal-
lucinate the haint.

I'd always been the one to discover them, all my dead pets:
    slouched (greenback frog)
    prone (tree frog)
    puffed, afloat, against filter's stream (puffers)
    capsized above garland of tailfin (betta, Cocytus)
    supine (the newt whose bath I drew too hot)
    right lateral recumbent (the dragon, Scrabblor, whose scales
        squashed along the glass)[1]

---

[1] This would be Grandma Bingo's last posture too, her body pinned between
her bed and the wall the day after Christmas, as if she had been searching for
the pores of her habitat.

Some pets died, and I only knew it because when I prodded them with a stick, their eyes simply stayed shut (leopard gecko). Sometimes, I prodded and they blinked: the indignant eye stalks of the hermit crab. *Not yet*, it signaled. Some were buried. Most were flushed.

By 2006, Chaleido was among the last survivors of my doleful menagerie. He had lost his juvenile appetite, and the substrate writhed with gut-loaded crickets. Zach, the plainspoken lizard expert at Burton's Total Pet, sold me powder to stimulate Chaleido's appetite and casually explained the *veiled* chameleon hailed from Saudia Arabia, not Madagascar like I kept insisting. For so long, I had pretended that square foot enclosure was of African isle, natural and tropic. Chaleido was my nineteenth pet, yet I was still botching the FAQs. I returned home to his fraudulent habitat and waited for him to feast. At night, I heard the tongue surge in the dark, skewering crickets and whispering satiation.

Satisfied, I sidled the stairs for midnight Nutty Bars. Grandma Bingo was in the dark kitchen too: sitting on a stool, eating handfuls of dog food. Rather than correct her, we sat at the counter, munching our respective snacks: my teeth, her gums champing, champing. A gulp. Maybe a smile. It was not, as Mom wanted to suggest, passive aggression. *She'd rather eat dog food than my food?* The physician finally explained that gustatory deficits were common at her age. "If she really enjoys it, let it be. Still plenty of nutrients in dog food."

Upstairs, Dad's CPAP whooshed. His nostrils gulped after liters of oxygen. It was a strange time for him; there had been an inversion in which he became his keeper's keeper, in which his keep kept a chameleon. With the usual caretaking flowchart redistributed, no one thought to ask: Who now is keeping Dad?

The doctors overprescribed. The side effects and symptoms

combined. Sleep apnea, insomnia, diabetic neuropathy, carpal tunnel, joint replacements. Dad pilfered brochures from the offices, reading up on the enigmatic syndromes, disorders, conditions he might (one day) have. When one retires as young as he did, the mind still mid-career, hypochondriasis becomes its own job description. No longer punching the clock, his days remained unpunctuated. He web surfed until sunset and slept until 3 PM, often wearing the same loose-fitting outfit for two, three days consecutively.

Occasionally, Dad entered my room to bottle-spray the chameleon's leaves, mesh, and substrate to humidify and hydrate. He got a kick out of it, the way the cool water changed Chaleido's coloration. We watched the beads on the veil collapse under their own weight before converging into a trickle that skirted the green skull. Because my bedroom was the warmest in the house, Dad sometimes turned the bottle on himself and spritzed his forehead and pits. Dad gave the lizard a thumbs up before departing. "You're alright, Chaleido." Chaleido, suspended on his tightrope vine, arms outstretched like a mime holding a barbell, blinked, blinked, blinked.

Toting its wardrobe internally in cell clusters, the chameleon is a deceptively naked old world lizard. Chaleido changed colors according to the thermostat autorun schedule, his chromatophores shifting to regulate his body temperature, sacs of pigment flashing brown (melanophore), blue (iridophore), yellow (xanthophore), and red (erythrophore). I wore all black.

Late at night, I would lean Chaleido's cage against the wall, retrieve the Ziploc snack bag I filled with Dad's amphetamines. I used to store contraband in the back of my amplifier (vibrating cock ring and bubble-gum-flavored lubricant), in the dropped ceiling (weed and pipe and roach clips), in picnic coolers and soccer cleats (ribbed condoms). All were eventually found, but this cavity beneath Chaleido's cage was safest of all since Mom always stayed way away from the reptiles.

By 2007, I regularly ingested an amphetamine before bed each night, vowing to be last awake. I stared in the mirror, drawing lines beneath my eyes with mom's black Avon eyeliner and coating my nails with black matte polish under Chaleido's flickering UVB light. And Chaleido, awake(ned), glared, probably peeved that I never used the dragon's bask lamp or the puffers' strip light. Why not sit cross-legged on the carpet, plug in the old lighthouse nightlight I'd retired to the sock drawer?

When my friend inherited his late grandfather's Penthouse trove, he knew he couldn't conceal the full library in his bedroom, so he created a rudimentary database, a subscription service he documented in a baseball scorebook. He loaned the mags out to his closest friends. For years, I had been smuggling naked pets into my room, storing them on nightstands; this new contraband, though—the prurient pages of the annual Pet of the Year issues—had to be kept underbed, where it awaited my irregular spans of attention.

I knew Chaleido couldn't see in the dark. Zach told me so. This deficit may be why I kept Chaleido's cage closest. For years, he heard my sheets rustling and could only wonder; the mysterious hand stroked in the dark as I extrapolated the day's cleavage into bare-chested fantasy. I self-fondled for many dark minutes, wondering which of my remaining pets had night vision. Who could see this ritual throttling? I sensed their collective blink in the periphery. When I started harboring the *Penthouses*, though, I masturbated with the aid of Chaleido's UVB light.

With painted nails, masturbation had the illusion of a hand job. It took a couple weeks to get over the intrusive illusion of my friend's late grandfather, his geriatric genitals. I concentrated extra hard on the glossy nipples and the painted nails on my left hand. For five minutes, sometimes more, I imagined it belonged to Nikie St. Gilles, Juliet Cariaga, or Paige Summers. If I didn't let the paint dry, I'd wake to polish on the penis, dried like a venereal mold. More than once, I had to carefully swab it with the acetone remover. If I was too distracted, I'd discontinue and stare at Chaleido whose insouciant eyes whirled as if he hadn't seen a thing.

When a magazine's due date neared, I scored the best images with an X-ACTO knife, carefully extracting and caching them in the inconspicuous pages of the only oversized book I owned: *The Real Mother Goose*. When I closed the book, I imagined the voracious Peter-Peter Pumpkin Eater's jaws gorging on Andi Sue Irwin's thighs or the Cat's fiddle ("Hey, diddle diddle—") bowing Sunny Leone's limbs.

In the years leading up to that first (and only) time I had sex in my childhood bedroom, you could find me in the movie the-atre's handicap seats, the cramped bathroom in the basement where spiders gnawed our ankles, the backseats of cars parked in baseball fields' gravel lots, and especially on the product-de-fected "Tony's Got It!" mattress that I dragged over a half-mile to the alcove in the woods dubbed Verona, where once a fellow trespasser heard the shifty humping and lifted his rifle, aiming for deer, peering through 18x zoom night-vision scope ready to count the antlers, discovering our teenage fuck instead of an eight-point buck, his voyeur eye squinting, squinting into the optics for a few lingersome moments at our wilderness pornog-raphy.

When we were finally home alone (a rarity because my Dad's disability kept him in bed, in house most days of the week), I noticed my girlfriend's discomfort, her gritted teeth, and I asked what was wrong. Apparently, she was alarmed that Chaleido was watching us. I quickly covered his cage with a bath towel, but there were others—the puffers, the dragon—so we stopped. Bedroom sex would have to wait until college, where there the

University of Pittsburgh had "a strict no-pet policy within the residence halls and on campus apartments."

In college, I was insomnious—either because of the amphetamines or because my routine had been disrupted; I had become accustomed to Chaleido's proximity, his blind hovering. I brought an empty cage to my single dorm—equipped it with substrate, a rock dish, and vines—a conceptual pet simulation that twice stymied my RA who was eager to write citations. I kept the lid off the empty cage, which gave the illusion that a pet had just escaped, that maybe it was still there in the room. I even named my fugitive pet Kimble.

When Chaleido died, I got a curt phone call from Dad. Grandma Bingo had died just months prior, and it seemed wrong to act like the chameleon's death was of any consequence to me. Dad didn't say (and I didn't ask) what he'd do with the chameleon's corpse. Later that month, at an off-campus party, someone sang a variation of the Bingo folk song ("B-I-N-G-O"). I glowered at him, nearly picked a fight. Instead, I vacated the party, drunk and maudlin. Back in my dormitory, I twisted the beads of Grandma's rosary. Peering through the loop as if into a tomb, I waited for Chaleido to emerge.

Eight years later, as I help Dad plant Chinese maple saplings in the backyard, the post-hole digger clamping and turning the earth a few feet away from our own unmarked pet cemetery— the Yorkies, canary, and water dragon—I finally ask him, "Did you end up burying Chaleido?" but he can't remember. I ask a few more times, trying different syntaxes, hoping something will trigger his recall, but he continues his work, massaging the flexible pot to dislodge the base cylinder of soil. I clamp earth for hours as grasshoppers leap. In the evening, I sit on the porch railing, staring at the sapling silhouettes, listening to summer crickets' strange chirp. I think Chaleido probably had too much girth to be flushed.

If I turned his bones in the yard.
Misfits: *They called us walking corpses*
If I sat among his resurrection's clone.
Descendents: *Got up on the wrong side of life*
If I stirred the chromatophores onto the foreground.
NOFX: *And on to the floor / my closest friend*
Then Chaleido: may you ever iridesce.

Of No Ground:
Late Days In the Country of Eighteen Tides

1. *Once, up on the alluvial banks of the mudflat, we gathered to watch the water rise.*

2. An essay may begin "Once upon" when it takes as its subject: time. Or, in the case of this essay, "Once, up_on" is a way to begin writing about an historical topography, a text that reminisces about past elevations. No longer a naïve commencement for fictions (in Bengali, it goes "*Ek deshe chhilo…*" meaning "In some country, there was…"), "Once, up_on" jettisons nostalgia for fact: a sinking land is a shrinking land.

3. Seated on a bus en route to the southern Bangladeshi river port of Khulna, I am offered a newborn. "Please hold?" I am asked. It's been awhile since I've held a baby, and it shows. She groans at my lack of confidence, bucking her head against the slack geometry of my cradle arms. The bus climbs the ramp to a ferry slip and parks. The bus driver thrusts the handle, and the door opens. One of the ferrymen doubles as muezzin as he calls the passengers to *Asr* prayer. The bus driver is beneath me now, kneeling on the cement margin between bus and ferry rail. He is kneeling and then he is prostrate. In time, he is kneeling again. He is synchronized with his passengers, all oriented toward the port-side qiblah. I hoist the restless baby to the window, hoping that if she sees her praying grandfather, she will settle.

Our aerial view of a dozen bowed scalps, many covered by identical knit skullcaps, renders him indistinguishable. The ferry moves at eighteen knots, floating across the swift convergence of the Padma and Jamuna Rivers. When I look away from the window, I feel it flowing into my left shoulder. I watch the baby, her fluttery lashes dark as if brushed with mascara.

4. A Bangladeshi newborn has a life expectancy of seventy years, meaning this one might just barely outlast the drowning land in which she was born. Projection is genre-neutral. Consider the meteorologist's "80% chance of precipitation." Only time will tell if it's just hydrohyperbolism.

5. I arrived in Bangladesh on January 21, 2015 just as the 114th United States Congress voted on a slew of amendments to S.1, the Keystone XL Pipeline Act. After a decade of congressional infighting about the reality of climate change, senators agreed to vote on an amendment that would, once and for all, "express the sense of Congress regarding climate change." Ninety-eight senators concurred "climate change is real and not a hoax." Mississippi Senator Roger Wicker was the sole politician who managed to steel his denial.

6. This amendment means that, as an American, I no longer sound like a hypocrite when I ask questions about climate change: *How* far up_on? (i.e., Δ meters?), *How* past was "once"? (i.e., Δ years?).

7. The grandfather returns with a deep smile embedded in his facial hair. The oranges he peels are made invisible by the backdrop of saffron beard. He drops the zest into the bus aisle among shattered peanut shells. The citric scent is a temporary reprieve from the ubiquitous brine of fish carcass and body odor. He trades me a peeled orange for the return of his granddaughter. Many kilometers later, even after the bus has sped away from the riverbank, my arms continue to perfect the cradle, now only holding an iPod.

8. Every fifteen minutes, the bus passes through a village or bazaar. Undulating crowds follow a man—there's one in every village—who spits political vitriol through a megaphone. Collec-

tively, they are trying to impose a transportation blockade across Bangladesh by firebombing busses, lorries, and boats, even derailing passenger trains. A man thumps the aluminum beneath my window with an umbrella. Earlier, men who had been shoveling rubble onto the train tracks, hurled rocks at us. The driver divides the crowds with a continuous blow from the air horn.

Elsewhere, in Dhaka, the opposition leader of the Bangladesh National Party (BNP), Khaleda Zia, is confined to her office. Security forces have formed a cordon at all exits, awaiting Zia's reversal of the debilitating *hartal*. After two sleepless nights in a guesthouse on Dhaka University's campus—a couple floors above the flinging of Molotov cocktails and hand grenades—I am much looking forward to the isolation of the mangrove forest.

9. On either side of the road to Khulna (the port of embarkation), tubewells and low-lift pumps burst water over green paddies. Agricultural workers bundle jute stems in fields lined with coconut palms. Near Mollahat, the driver stops for fuel. From my window, I see two Bangladeshi boys swimming in a pond. The older boy dunks the other—a brother or friend. The smaller boy disappears through the surface of the water for an uncomfortable interval. I hold my own breath as I wait for him to emerge. The younger boy wails, begins wading toward the bank for escape, but the older boy makes a convincing apology. They stay in the pond, and I watch them skeptically. From the bus window, my vantage is that of a lifeguard stand. After three summers as an ocean lifeguard, the impulse to blow a whistle at the older boy has become automated. I remove my emergency whistle from my camera case, let it dangle from my fingers. Whistle is a universal language of alarm.

Once, I blew my whistle at a young father who was fake-drowning his son. "Were you whistling at ME?" he asked defensively. "Yessir," I said with public servant assertiveness. "We can't have that. You two may just be going through the motions of drowning, but from here, I'm obliged to treat it like the real thing." The son nodded at me, grateful I think.

By the time the bus engine starts, the Bangladeshi boys are water wrestling again. The younger boy is dunked repeatedly like a biscuit into tea, becoming soggier with each dip. I open the window, put the whistle to my lips, and cup the cavity. I hesitate long enough to remember the baby asleep next to me.

"You can't hesitate," my lieutenant had told me during my one and only whistle-blowing lesson (Day 1 of Rehoboth Beach Patrol). "When it comes to another person's life, there's nothing wrong with a false alarm." The bus leaves the station, and residual air peeps through the whistle. The palms, the pond, the boys all disappear.

10. Bangladesh, size of Iowa, has a population half that of the United States. During monsoon, the deluge saturates the water table. The landmass shrinks to Louisiana proportions, and farmers flee to the megacity capital, Dhaka.

11. Over half of Dhaka's seven million people dwell in the slum complex. The number is expected to triple by the end of the century as climate change continues to accelerate urbanization. Days before, walking through an interminable corridor, a man asked me, "Come from?" I crouched to see inside his aluminum walls—a scant fifty square feet of shadow, crushed brick, and limbs. Flanked by two bashful daughters who clung to his biceps, the man asked again. "Where come from?" It was a gender-inverted replica of Dorothea Lange's *Migrant Mother*. "America," I say. "U-S-A?" he verifies. I nod. "Where do *you* come from?" My reciprocal question is met with reticence. I know he is likely a domestic climate refugee. "We say it is not there anymore," the man says. "It does not exist anymore. For us, it does not exist." *Ek deshe chhilo…*

12. "It's too late for us… and so we are the canary," said i-Kiri-bati President Tong. It is a powerful metaphor when considering the canary's sacrificial utility in service to coalmining, the same fossil fuel that has exacerbated sea-level rise in atoll nations like Kiribati or Maldives. The latter's average elevation is 1.5 meters (about the height of Danny DeVito). At least when the land disintegrates, though, a *canary* can take flight.

13. As the United Nations hesitates to redefine refugee, Earth's lowest-lying people (ni-Vanuatu, Tuvaluan, et al.) watch the water rise: SOMEONE WHO, OWING TO A WELL-FOUND-ED FEAR OF BEING [DROWNED] FOR REASONS OF [TOPOGRAPHY], IS OUTSIDE OF THE [DESH] OF HIS NATIONALITY, AND IS UNABLE TO, OR OWING TO SUCH FEAR, IS UNWILLING TO AVAIL HIMSELF OF THE PROTECTION OF THAT [DESH].

14. Desh as in "country" as in "my [desh] 'tis of thee" as in "ask not what your [desh] can do for you, but what you can do for your [desh] (and/or another [desh])" as in Bangla-desh, the country where they speak Bangla, the –desh which seems to get bigger and bigger, each passing kilometer, my bus-window-blink odometer, but in fact, the –desh whose centimeters annu-ally vanish with the encroachment of its eighteen tides. I arrive in Khulna at sunset.

15. I board the R. B. Emma just as the time-obsessed *muezzin* calls from his mosque minaret. Solo fishermen, who had been careering toward the market, let their oars flatten against the sides of their rowboats. They kneel to pray *Maghrib* as their boats are reversed by the current, drifting away from destination, bob-bing in the wake of the southward barges on the Rupsha River.

16. The Sundarbans tour begins at low tide. It's blue hour, and the silhouette guide introduces himself as Emu. He gestures to the captain and the cook, and finally to the only other tourist

aboard, an eminently reasonable Australian named Bruce.

17. The last time I tried to make this trip in May of 2013, it was postponed due to the arrival of Cyclone Mahasen. "CNN says 200,000 people are in the process of evacuating Southern Bangladesh," my mother relayed. "Why go to a place everyone else is trying to leave?" When flights over the Bay of Bengal were cancelled, I was forced to remain in Myanmar's Inle Lake.

18. In "Imaginary Homelands," Salman Rushdie writes:
> It may be argued that the past is a country from which we have all emigrated, that its loss is part of our common humanity. The writer who is out-of-country and even out-of-language may experience this loss in an intensified form…

The loss of a homeland as vast as past creates a global diaspora; who, since before Mayan *haab*, has ever lived outside of time? I imagine a quartz mechanism compelling a massive second hand to sweep over a canvas world map, each second expatriating us over and over again. Rushdie's case for "once up_on" privileges the visitor because of her "physical discontinuity…" which enables her "to speak properly and concretely on a subject of universal significance and appeal." After years of unsurety, the needling anxiety of my outsider-in relation to the subject matter of Bangladesh—nearly forfeiting my pen to TSA along with my box cutters, ice picks, and meat cleavers—Rushdie so casually extends license to the visitor. It's a visa that always and never expires.

19. I am constantly reminding myself that I am not just visiting a place, but also a moment.

20. The captain points across the starboard deck to a random whirlpool beneath our ship. I think he is simply trying to point out the cross-current waters, but he's emphatic that I keep watching. Eventually, a dolphin emerges from the eddy. Air

gusts from the nostril on top of its head. "Susu," the captain says, an onomatopoeia.

21. Dusk now, the boat still streaking toward the forest, the captain turns on the generator. I am beneath the deck in a cozy cabin, sipping tea as the generator's propane fumes diffuse through the air. Emu visits with a map of the Sundarbans, more detailed than the ones I'd ever clicked through on Google. He touches his fingertips to our many awaiting destinations, scooting it along the Rupsha River, which becomes the Passur. "We'll drop the anchor around here tonight," he says, his finger jittering over Mongla, the last fishing village before the reserve. Beneath Mongla, he pokes at distributaries, channels leading to forest stations. He taps a sea beach, a watchtower, islands and coast guard stations, and most southerly, coastal grasslands overlooking the Bay of Bengal. I pump hot water over a used tea sachet while Emu nestles in his mattress. I study the map, which, without Emu's guiding finger, becomes cryptic again. I am perplexed by the plasticity of its myriad channels. The tides swell even within the paper's gloss. The Captain turns off the generator without warning, and I sleep alongside the baffling map.

22. I wake several times to the boat's mild bob. We're above the silt bed anchor and below dark zenith. Through a sliver of window I've kept open, I see the articulation of familiar constellations. And yet, the previous nights' insomnia lingers. During the 1975 Bangladesh Liberation War, Secretary of State Henry Kissinger called Bangladesh a "basket case," and since then, this one-off remark has been used repeatedly as a litmus test for the state of governance in the country. I recall the man who wielded an umbrella beneath my bus window, his gritted teeth and heavy thump. It's the stuff of political satire—the obsolescence of the umbrella, now reassigned as a weapon for a fraught *political* climate only. I imagine the battered umbrella in the corner of his bedroom now, his wife's wide eyes as he snores.

23. The captain's wristwatch tracks the tides. We anchor at Mon-ghla before midnight, where the captain sets his alarm. The channels that are sealed at low tide reopen when it's high.

24. During those summers in Delaware, I informally studied the Atlantic Ocean from the lifeguard stand, contemplating climate change. Twice a day, the changing tide triggered the delusion that this could be it—the spontaneous (not incremental) incur-sion of sea-level rise. Beyond my limited horizon, I sensed the apocalyptic calving of freshwater glaciers, the melt-and-gush of ice caps, a continent in a state of retreat due to greenhouse ra-diation.

25. The Gangotri Glacier, one of three primary sources for the headwaters of the Ganges River, rises up to 7000 meters. From peak (see Δ as mountain) to bay (see Δ as delta), there is a finite difference (see Δ as 'change in') of 7000 meters. The snowmelt trickles from the Himalayas to the Sundarbans (equivalent of Winnipeg to Juarez).

26. Hiking notes on flora+fauna of Sundarbans: ...*six-smooth coated otters jouncing on the riverbank, single-file, muzzling through water. Kingfisher flits above... Spotted deer stand ass-to-ass-to-ass-to-ass, hooves stuck in the alluvium of new accretion. They bolt and break... The forest ranger balances a rifle on his shoulder... Rhesus macaques climb through mangrove apple trees. Branches flex into parabolas, crack, and fall... Fif-teen-foot crocodile (2x Shaq) stirs from his bask and dives from the bank to pass our bow. I see the milky membrane over his right eye. I want Bruce to proclaim "Crikey!" in his Aussie accent, but he doesn't... Dry tiger scat near orange-striped phoenix palm... Brahminy kite swoops... Dry pug marks (adult tiger)... Red-whiskered bulbul... Black drongo... Massive orange beak of the brown-winged kingfisher... Egret's zipline landing onto treetop... Chef cracks crab claws with a knife, playful torture... White sand shimmers with mica. Trees grow on beach, form dense canopy. Forest ends abruptly on a private beach on the Bay of Bengal, its sand dimpled by sand-bubbler crabs. Industrious, they purloin thousands of tiny sand pellets.*

27. The clay road to the village is lined with date palms, tapped, their brown sap flowing into jars. Bruce, a schoolteacher with a small cattle farm in New South Wales, is curious about the beel. "What do they grow?" he asks Emu. Emu asks the nearest farmer, a middle-aged Hindu man, who explains, "Nothing right now. Next season, rice only." Since the tides have risen, there is salt in the water table. To exacerbate this, India diverts the Ganges' freshwater flow just fifteen kilometers before it reaches Bangladesh, fluming it into the feeder canals of the Farakka Barrage. "How do farmers survive on a fallow field?" Bruce asks. Without asking the farmer, Emu already knows. "Microloans."

We pass a boy who leans over a corkscrewing medusa of black eels. Mulched hay sticks to their black leather skin. He chops one into pink cross-sections, dropping its segments like licorice onto a dark bed of ribbons.

28. The farmer invites us onto his property. His daughter slides a plastic chair behind me. A caged mynah named Moynah cuckoos then laughs. It even cries like a baby. The farmer's daughter climbs a ladder into a tree and drops kul and guava into a basket. She sets the basket at my feet and sits at a century-old treadle. I nibble slowly at the small fruit.

29. I ask the farmer's mother, Geeta, "How long have you lived here?" She nods at Emu's translation before replying, "Over two hundred years." I instinctively look at Geeta's bony hands, tangled with blue veins, as if this is where her age must be concentrated. She is no supercentenarian. Rather, Geeta assumed the 'you' of my question was collective, historical.

"I was born here when it was East Pakistan," Geeta says. "Before the liberation." Her dada-shoshur (grandfather-in-law), born sometime before the nineteenth century, was a jute farmer for the British East India Company. And his grandfather, she implies, was born in this very village when the Mughal Empire sprawled over the territory. "We will always live here," she says confidently.

30. Ritwik Ghatak's film, *A River Called Titas* (1973), is dedicated to "the myriad of toilers of ever-lasting Bengal," and yet here, where Bengalis must let their fields go fallow, the toil seems to discontinue.

31. I gaze over the beel, listening to the girl's ankles pliant on the treadle, the wheel's slow whir. I listen to nothing being spun. The village has endured empire, colony, partition, and a volatile transition into democracy. The farmer cues Moynah to laugh and cry and laugh again, consecutively. The emotional gamut is entertaining.

"Have they ever considered leaving? Going to Khulna? Or Dhaka?" I ask with an air of inevitability. The farmer waits for a translation, but Emu politely refuses, shaking his head at me.

32. Geeta leads us to the shrine of Bonbibi. Passing through a gate, we huddle beneath a beehive. Strings of tinsel cascade from thatch roof. Potted plants simulate a jungle backdrop behind the figurine. "Bonbibi willing," Geeta says.

33. There will be a last Bangladeshi. She who stands up_on the peak of Mowdok Mual will earn the esteem of last citizen. Imagine census as roll call: "I remain," a declaration of last presence. Then what? Ankle deep in saline water, subaqua desh will dissolve her into flotsam émigré.

34. In the early 1900s, my great-grandfather, Gustaf, repaired countless hopper cars for the shaft-entry colliery in my hometown. I worry that our coalmining legacy has impelled the unrecoverable theft of Bangladesh.

35. Bangladesh ends at Kotka Khal, the wide-open cliff on the Bay of Bengal. A few miles away, a small char (island) rises from the water, punctuating the contiguous borders. We climb out of our boat, walking the pier backwards as we watch the stunning terminus at sunset. I peer into the viscera of the confiscated nowkas beneath us, boats forfeited to the coast guard. They had disintegrated into long ribcages in the beach grass, their limp rudders left untouched for many seasons. We are greeted by an older man, a muezzin, whose saffron beard flows over his blue sweatshirt. He has just finished eating and alternates between chatting with Emu and plucking his gums with a long finger-nail. He seems adrenalized by our company as he leads us past a mosque and grass huts to a pond then a well then a vista. He bounces before us, performing calisthenics and stretching. There will be a volleyball game after *Maghrib*, he tells us: forest officials versus coast guards officers.

35. The muezzin points to the knurled earth uprooted by wild boars. He points into a well, at a *ghat* and hoof prints. He plucks boroi from a tree and points at our mouths. Bruce and I nibble the sour fruit. The muezzin points at cards strewn at a campsite, cryptically at the eight of spades. He picks his teeth, and with a chunk of food still on the nail, he points at the tail feathers of a drongo. To point is to reveal. It becomes an ecstatic gesture, a skewering of the mundane. I start to think he's making fun of us, providing fodder for the esoteric perception of the eco-tourist. The next time he points (at a porcupine quill), my vision doesn't follow the implicit leash.

I walk away from the muezzin, Emu, and Bruce and enter the camp where migrant grass cutters have left behind broken cas-settes. Ribbons of magnetic tape are unspooled onto dead em-bers, the mute ghazals of Pankaj Udhas. Each step into the camp is premeditated as I use the playing cards as steppingstones to avoid hidden chain vipers. This game of call bridge has been abandoned, the migrants now working elsewhere. Only a few feet above sea level, their coastal labor in these slouching huts will be unbidden in the coming years when the grassy port to the maze goes underwater. It will all become an undulant pasture in a shallow bay, and eels (not snakes) will wend through these reeds.

36. We stand with the young officers of the Bangladesh Coast Guard before leaving. A clean-shaven man holds a volleyball as the others look into the Bay. I ask if they've heard anything on the radio about the hartal, if the roads are safe again, if Khaleda Zia has emerged from her office. But a voice booms from the mosque. *Maghrib*. The clean-shaven man sets the volleyball on the ground, and they leave us behind. A wild boar sniffs at an oil drum as we cross the pier.

37. Emu points southwest across the Bay of Bengal. "This is the end of Bangladesh," Emu says with unintentional gravitas. "Out there," he says, "is Swatch of No Ground."

Here is where the world's largest delta yields the world's largest deep-sea fan. The Ganges and Brahmaputra Rivers deposit Himalayan sediment into the basin, creating turbidity currents that form expansive canyons, the deepest of which is Swatch of No Ground (SONG).

Swarming with turtles, porpoises, dolphins, sharks, and eight species of whale, it seems an apt future capital city for all the imperiled island states, which will (soon enough) be veritable swatches of no ground too.

38. If we believe Rushdie's claim that the past psychically diasporizes all people, then it should be no surprise that climate will physically do the same. Climatology is, after all, an interval study of our atmospheric past.

39. Until we invite them to live among us, it seems we'll just

watch them dredge rocks for artificial islands. Watch them affix cinder blocks to scant terra using gull shit mortar. Watch as the post-Edenic landfills are molded into neo-Thilafushis. Watch engineers unload monuments of rubbish from freighters—the polystyrene avalanche of packing peanuts interspersed with java K-cups and soiled Huggies, snapped coat hangers and used plastic cutlery. Please watch this ever-lasting toil for as long as it lasts.

Acknowledgments

Thanks to all of my English teachers. Miss Charlene, first of all. Thanks forever to Jennifer Boyd, Brian Fleckenstein, Patrick MacLaughlin, and Renny Thompson. Hail to Pitt, hail to: Toi Derricotte, Sherrie Flick, Jeff Martin, Jeff Oaks, Irina Reyn, Gayle Rogers, Uma Satyavolu, and Philip E. Smith.

Thanks, my mentors of the low desert: Kate Bernheimer, Chris Cokinos, Elizabeth Evans, Alison Hawthorne-Deming, Ander Monson, Manuel Muñoz, Suresh Raval, Aurelie Sheehan, and Joshua Marie Wilkinson.

Thanks, my colleagues of the high desert: Jane Armstrong, Justin Bigos, Erin Stalcup, Nicole Walker, Allen Woodman.

IOU, friends: Lewis DeJong. Colin Hodgkins. Mike Powell. Sarah Minor! Thomas Mira y Lopez. Cory Aaland. Dave Mondy. Vontaze. Paige Pinkston. Will Slattery. Jess Langan-Peck. Melissa Gutierrez. Ben Rybeck. Ted McLoof. Craig Reinbold.

Time-tested: TRP. Gianni Label. Molly Green. Sohit Kanotra.

Your support mattered: Amanda Nelson. Brittany Bankovich. Colleen McIlroy.

Thanks to the editors of the following journals (and habitual guest reader, Jill Talbot) in which these essays originally appeared: *Wag's Revue, Alaska Quarterly Review, Prairie Schooner, Sundog Lit, Fourth Genre, Guernica Daily, BOAAT, Passages North, Fourteen Hills, JuxtaProse* and *Terrain.org.*

Thanks to Dr. Fakrul Alam of Dhaka University, Md. Abdul Awal Miah of the Asiatic Society of Bangladesh, and Md. Emamul "Emu" Hossein of The Guide Tours Ltd. Thanks to Scott Russell Sanders for selecting "Of No Ground: Late Days in the Country of Eighteen Tides" as the winner of the "6th Annual Creative Nonfiction Award: (Dis)placement" at *Terrain. org*.

Thanks, Jon Roemer, for taking hold of these pages and editing them. Also, for letting us lodge large in the cottage.

Thanks (again) to Ander Monson, the 119th element. My gratitude will never expire.

Andie Francis, you're irreplaceable. Thanks for your patiences, big and small.

To all my pets—flushed, buried, or alive: I wasn't an only child after all. Thank you. To Arni especially, who sits on my shoulder, always my first reader.

How do you do it, Mom & Dad? I love you.

About the author

Lawrence Lenhart's writing has appeared or is forthcoming in *Alaska Quarterly Review*, *Fourth Genre*, *Greensboro Review*, *Gulf Coast*, *Passages North*, *Prairie Schooner*, *Western Humanities Review*, and elsewhere. His essay "The Well-Stocked and Gilded Cage" won *Prairie Schooner's* 2016 Virginia Faulkner Award for Excellence in Writing, "Of No Ground: Late Days In the Country of Eighteen Tides" earned *Terrain's* 6th Annual Creative Nonfiction Award, and "Give Me That For Nothing, Now I Am Going Away" was selected as a notable essay in Best American Essays 2015. Lenhart is a lecturer of fiction and creative nonfiction at Northern Arizona University and a reviews editor and assistant fiction editor of *DIAGRAM*. He studied writing at the University of Pittsburgh and earned his MFA from the University of Arizona, where he received two Foundation Awards and the biennial LaVerne Harrell Clark Award.

CPSIA information can be obtained at www.ICGtesting.com
Printed in the USA
BVOW08s0209080916

461415BV00005B/143/P

Five essays on pets
—a dog, a bird, a tortoise,
a ferret, and a chameleon—
anchor this wild menagerie,
exploring childhood spirituality,
global positioning systems,
wildlife conservation,
and climate change.

"At the least unhinged and quite possibly
a little insane, Lawrence Lenhart's essays
are perverse in the best way, willing to
sacrifice whatever (self-protection, sleep,
comfort, love, safety, tradition) in search of
the weird heart beating inside the world.
Lenhart's a legitimate threat: a yearner
and a quester. Ain't no cage, however
gilded, can hold this bird for long."

— Ander Monson
author of *Letter to A Future Lover*

"There are books with turtles in them.
And books with dogs. And books about bullies.
And books about hoarding birds. There are books
about Bangladesh and books about the end of the
world but I do not think there is another book that
pulls back the veil to reveal how woven together
dogs, bullies, birds, babies and Bangladesh are.
Lenhart does something in *The Well-Stocked and
Gilded Cage* that only someone with a special kind
of genius can do: train his focus as sharply inward
as he does outward. Intense awareness combined
with his intense concern make for a big heart and
a big brain and a big, as in important, book."

— Nicole Walker
author of *Micrograms*

ORIGINAL
PROVOCATIVE
READING

OUTPOST19

ISBN 978-1-944853
5

9 781944 853013

SO-DZX-638